A Willi... ...Book

Creating Clever Castles & Cars

from Boxes and Other Stuff

Kids ages 3-8 make their own pretend play spaces

● Mari Rutz Mitchell ●

Illustrations by Michael Kline

Williamson Books
Nashville, Tennessee

Library of Congress Cataloging-in-Publication Data

Mitchell, Mari Rutz.
    Creating clever castles & cars (from boxes and other stuff): kids ages 3–8 make their own pretend play spaces / Mari Rutz Mitchell ; illustrations by Michael Kline.
        p. cm. — (A Williamson Little Hands book)
    Includes index.
    ISBN 0-8249-6783-6 (case bound : alk. paper) — ISBN 0-8249-6782-8 (softcover : alk. paper)
    1. Handicraft—Juvenile literature. I. Kline, Michael P. II. Title. III. Series.
    TT160.M52 2006
    745.5—dc22

        2005028040

Little Hands® series editor: **Susan Williamson**
Project editor: **Vicky Congdon**
Interior design and illustrations: **Michael Kline**
Cover design and illustration: **Michael Kline**

Published by Williamson Books
An imprint of Ideals Publications
535 Metroplex Drive, Suite 250
Nashville, Tennessee 37211
www.idealsbooks.com
800-586-2572

Printed and bound in China.
All rights reserved.
10 9 8 7 6 5 4 3 2 1

Dedication

For children who love to build! For my own kids, who daily set sail in their "chair boat," saving whales and steering clear of sharks. And to my husband, who enthusiastically shipped those same kids off to faraway islands on the weekends, so I could hide in my cardboard office!

Acknowledgments

Thanks to all the little architects who helped build projects and to Susan, Vicky, Michael, and Leslie, whose work made this book come alive! Thanks also to Miriam Easton Rutz, whose encouragement is never-ending.

CONTENTS

WELCOME HOME! 11
HOUSES & LIVING SPACES
  Cozy Cardboard House 12
  Flower Fairy House 15
  A-Frame House 18
  Adobe House 21
  Nesting Houses 24
  "Roomy" Cardboard House 26
  "Icy" Igloo 28
  Newspaper-Roll Hut 31

COME RIGHT IN! 35
FAVORITE BUILDINGS & STRUCTURES
  Little Red Barn 36
  Big Stone Castle 39
  Clock Tower 42
  Pointed Pyramid 44

WHO LIVES HERE? 47
ANIMAL HOMES & HABITATS
  Spider Web 48
  Wiggly-Worm Tunnel 50
  Underground Burrow 52
  Bird's Nest 54
  Beaver Lodge 57
  Forest Log 60
  Anthill 62

LET'S GET MOVING! 65
ALL KINDS OF THINGS THAT GO
  Tricycle Taxi 66
  Bathtub Submarine 68

  Cruising Car 70
  Fire Engine 73
  Dump Truck 76
  Traveling Train 79
  High-Flying Helicopter 82
  Pirate Ship 84
  Rocking Boat 86
  Soaring Spaceship 88
  Front-End Loader 91
  Canoe 94
  Covered Wagon 97
  All-Aboard Bus 100

WHAT'S FOR SALE? 103
SHOPS & STANDS
  Ice-Cream Cart 104
  Roadside Stand 106
  General Store 108

ON WITH THE SHOW! 111
MINI-THEATERS & PLACES TO PERFORM
  Doorway Theater 112
  Circus Tent 115
  Corner Stage 118
  Marionette Theater 120
  Two-Box Theater 122

RESOURCES 125

INDEX 126

Imagine, Create & Play!

Ready to be an inventor, a builder, and a decorator? With some simple items and a little imagination, you can design and make all sorts of fun places to play. Create your own cardboard houses, animal homes, a general store, even a circus tent. How about all kinds of vehicles that zoom, roar, float, or blast off? Once you begin building, you open the door into an imaginary world where you can be just about anything, from a race-car driver to a magical princess on her throne to a pirate at the helm of a ship. Curl up like a hibernating bear in a cozy den or swim like a beaver into your very own lodge!

You'll be surprised by how easy it is to gather the things you need to build — they're all around you! The pictures and directions in this book will get you started. Then let your imagination fill in the rest.

You can add all sorts of personal touches, too, such as curtains or a mailbox for your house or dashboard buttons for your car.

Sometimes you might not have exactly what's called for. No problem — you can be even more creative and improvise by using what's handy instead. You're only minutes away from creating your very own amazing play spaces — so let's get started!

Mari

Why Encourage Kids to Play?

Who doesn't remember spending rainy days "traveling" aboard a cardboard-box rocket ship, performing a puppet show on a homemade stage, or hiding in a fort made of couch cushions? Early imaginative and pretend-play experiences like these are vital to every child's learning and development.

Increasingly, children are spending time in front of passive forms of entertainment such as video games and television. This book offers parents and teachers an alternative: more than 50 opportunities to engage children in open-ended and interactive architecture projects. These easy and imaginative activities encourage both dramatic and constructive play, essential elements of a child's cognitive, physical, and social development.

Through *constructive play* (play with a goal in mind, like building something), children learn elements of math, physics, and science. They develop small and large motor

skills. What's more, they have a satisfying end result to proudly display. In *dramatic play* (also known as symbolic, pretend, fantasy, make-believe, or imaginary play), children take on roles in which they pretend to be someone or something else. Engaging in dramatic play can have beneficial effects on a child's cognitive development, learning, and overall emotional well-being. When they engage in these types of play with other children, they increase their vocabulary and improve language skills. They also practice sharing and negotiation skills, thus improving peer relationships.

My belief is that children learn best through play, and that their environment has a direct influence on the quality of that play. Trained as a landscape architect, I have always been interested in the environment and its impact on children. I've worked as both a playground designer and a garden designer, and when designing spaces for children, I look to them for inspiration. Their fanciful ideas and creative minds always surprise me. Why not let them built their own play spaces?

After completing a master's degree in design and environmental analysis as well as several observational studies on children's play, I've concluded that children *should* build their own play spaces. In my studies, when children were given appropriate materials (called "loose parts"), they immediately engaged in constructive play, followed by dramatic play.

This book is the product of what I have learned as a researcher and also as a mother of three. The activities make it easy to encourage kids to create their own pretend play spaces out of simple materials such as cardboard boxes, old sheets, and tape. With the sense of ownership, the children are fully engaged in the activity and they have a sense of control, which makes the learning that much more powerful and effective.

CHOOSING ACTIVITIES

To help you choose appropriate activities, look for one of the following icons with each one.

This activity uses very few materials and requires minimal cutting of cardboard. It has one or two steps and is typically completed quickly, especially if you use minimal finishing touches.

This activity may have more steps and requires more extensive cutting or detailing.

This activity involves several steps and/or more materials (some fairly messy). It may require some manual dexterity, such as rolling and taping newspaper tubes or applying papier-mâché strips.

BEFORE YOU START

● **Let the child choose.** Kids will be much more excited about a project that they choose or have interest in. The more kids engage in the project, the better the results will be and the more they'll learn.

● **Do a little prep.** The more kids know about the subject matter, the more they'll be able to contribute ideas. Talk about the project, go on a field trip if possible, check out photos on the Internet, or read a book on the topic. Most of the activities include book recommendations; also, see RESOURCES on page 125.

BUILDING TIPS

 **IMPROVISE!**

● **Feel free to improvise!** The illustrations will help you visualize the directions, but remember: This book is only a guide. There are many ways to build any of these projects. Go ahead and make changes, improvise, and add to projects! Ask "How do you think we should make this?" I guarantee these young builders will continually amaze you with their creative ideas!

● **Hands off the finishing touches.** Decorating and adding accessories is where the kids can really shine — so let them! For safety reasons, you'll need to do the actual cutting of the cardboard boxes used in most of the projects (although kids can direct where they would like the doors and windows). Taking charge of the finishing touches offers kids the opportunity to be creative, as well as to personalize their projects and feel ownership of them.

● **Leave a project up for several days.** As time goes on, the activity will change, often becoming more complex as kids develop their dramatic play ideas. You'll notice that what starts out as a house becomes a post office the next day, a doctor's office the day after that, and so on. A car may grow wings and fly to the grocery store. Provide new or additional props based on the play scenarios.

SAFETY FIRST!

● **Keep little fingers away from sharp knives.** An adult should do all the cutting of cardboard, using a sharp utility knife.

● **When improvising with furniture, examine it first.** Check for sharp parts, splinters, exposed springs, etc. Cover any sharp points or hard surfaces with padding and/or duct tape.

● **Stay on the ground.** Children should not climb on top of  cardboard projects. Projects that fall apart easily are actually safer then those that are built to withstand the weight of a child.

● **Supervise use of rope and string.** Adults should supervise young children at all times when string or rope is used; kids should never wrap it around their bodies or necks.

● **Locate projects in safe areas.** Choose safe locations in open areas, avoiding areas of heavy traffic in the home or classroom.

● **Avoid small objects for children 3 and under.** Some of the materials listed in this book, such as bottle caps, are not appropriate for children who might put things in their mouths. Avoid these materials when working with very young children.

BASIC SUPPLIES

The materials used in this book are easy to find around the house or in the classroom. If you don't have a particular item handy, feel free to get creative (just keep safety in mind when substituting materials). Here is a list of the basic materials used for almost every project. For suggested materials to decorate and embellish your projects, see page 10.

✔ **Cardboard boxes, all sizes.** From appliance boxes and large moving cartons down to shoe boxes, and all sizes in between.

✔ **Poster board or stiff paper.** For signs, wheels, roofs, and other accessories.

✔ **Utility knife.** Use for cutting cardboard and other stiff materials. Make sure the blade is sharp and always cut on a large piece of cardboard or scrap wood to protect surfaces. Adult use only, please.

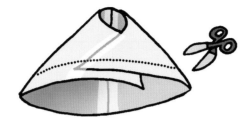

✔ **Scissors.** Child-safety scissors for cutting paper; craft scissors (for adult use) for cutting fabric, poster board, and other heavier materials.

✔ **Tape.** Use duct tape for building with and connecting heavy materials like cardboard or thick

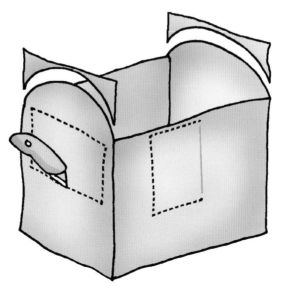

fabric. Note: it can strip wood finishes. Clear tape is fine when working with lighter-weight materials like construction paper, clear plastic, etc.

✔ **Glue.** White glue is easy to clean up and is great for gluing paper. A hot-glue gun (for adult use only) is better for gluing heavier materials, such as recyclables and other plastics.

✔ **Paint.** Use washable, nontoxic paints. For fun, try glitter or chalkboard paints.

ACCESSORIES

From a cereal-box oxygen pack for an astronaut to buttons and switches for a dashboard control panels, you'll have lots of creative fun using the items listed here to decorate and accessorize the basic projects. And the kids will come up with ways to use other items, too. Simply provide a variety of materials and let the kids be creative.

- ✔ Aluminum foil
- ✔ Aluminum pans
- ✔ Cardboard sheets (available at craft stores or recycling centers; or, cut a large box along the creases into sections)
- ✔ Cardboard six-pack carriers
- ✔ Cardboard tubes (from wrapping-paper, paper-towel, or toilet-paper rolls)
- ✔ Clear plastic or cellophane
- ✔ Cereal boxes
- ✔ Clementine boxes
- ✔ Coffee cans
- ✔ Computer keyboards (old or broken)
- ✔ Contact paper
- ✔ Fabric: old blankets, sheets, tablecloths, drapes, or other large pieces of material; fabric scraps

- ✔ Film canisters
- ✔ Flower pots
- ✔ Foam swim noodles
- ✔ Hula hoops
- ✔ Milk jugs
- ✔ Oatmeal containers
- ✔ Old CDs and cases
- ✔ Old kitchen pots and lids
- ✔ Newspaper
- ✔ Paper cups and plates
- ✔ Plastic bottles and caps
- ✔ Plastic containers
- ✔ String
- ✔ Tennis balls
- ✔ Thread spools
- ✔ Wallpaper scraps
- ✔ Yarn

Welcome Home!
Houses & Living Spaces

What does your house look like? Why do you think it looks that way? Houses look different, depending on where they are in the world and what building materials are handy. But these homes all have one thing in common: they are cozy spaces that provide a comfortable shelter.

Try building a variety of houses using all kinds of materials. Then decorate them to make them really feel like home!

Cozy Cardboard House

You and your stuffed animals will love settling into this comfortable little house. Don't forget to hang out the Welcome sign!

CHALLENGE LEVEL 1

Here's What You Need

✔ Large cardboard box
✔ Utility knife and scissors (for grownup use only)
✔ Empty plastic film canister
✔ Tape

FINISHING TOUCHES

Shoe box; real or pretend flowers; paint and paintbrushes; contact paper or construction paper; fabric scraps; old rug or section of carpeting

MAKE YOUR CARDBOARD HOUSE!

1. Place the box horizontally, open side down. Cut out doors and windows.

2. In the door, cut a circle to fit the film canister. Tape it in the hole.

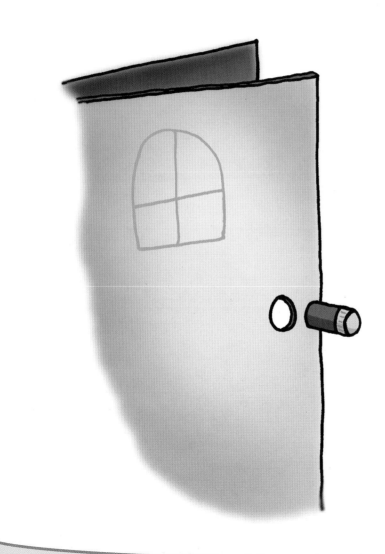

FINISHING TOUCHES

To add a windowbox for flowers, cut a hole the size of the shoe box just under the window and tape the box into the hole. Arrange the flowers in the box.

Paint the house. Add a house number and cut a mail slot in the front door.

Inside, decorate the walls with contact paper (or hang some of your own artwork!). Tape up pieces of fabric for curtains. Put down a rug.

MORE FUN!

COVER A CARDBOARD TUBE WITH FOIL FOR A FAUCET

● For a stove, cut an oven door in the front of a box.

ADD FILM-CANISTER KNOBS

PAINT ON BURNERS

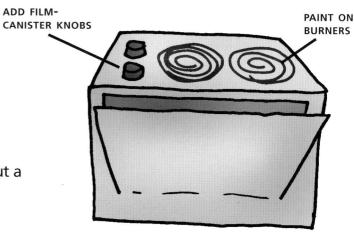

● To make a refrigerator, cut a door in a medium box.

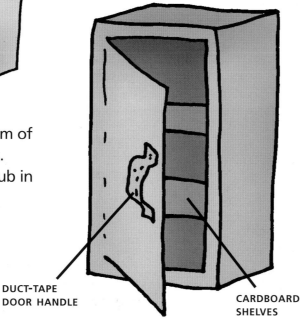

DUCT-TAPE DOOR HANDLE

CARDBOARD SHELVES

● To make a sink, trace the bottom of a plastic tub on top of a small box. Cut out the shape and place the tub in the hole.

Little Hands Story Corner™

How a House Is Built by Gail Gibbons
The Little House by Virginia Lee Burton
The Great Blue House by Kate Banks and Georg Hallensleben
This Is Our House by Michael Rosen

Flower Fairy House

Rest inside this big blossom — what a peaceful spot! If you're very quiet, a flower fairy just might visit!

Here's What You Need

✔ Scissors and string (for grownup use only)
✔ Hula hoop
✔ Tape
✔ Long pieces of lightweight fabric (floor to ceiling length)
✔ Cup hook

FINISHING TOUCHES

Fabric; ribbons; hot-glue gun (for grownup use only); silk flowers

Note to adults: When children play near hanging fabric, supervise at all times.

MAKE YOUR FAIRY HOUSE!

1. Tie three sections of string to the hula hoop as shown, an equal distance apart.

2. Tape the tops of the fabric strips around the hula hoop. Cut the bottoms in petal-like shapes.

3. Screw the cup hook into the ceiling. Attach the strings securely to the hook.

FINISHING TOUCHES

Decorate the top edge with a second piece of fabric. Tape long ribbons to the hula hoop so they hang down. Glue silk flowers all over.

MORE  FUN!

● What do you need to dress like a fairy? Wings, of course!

CUT WING SHAPE FROM CARDBOARD

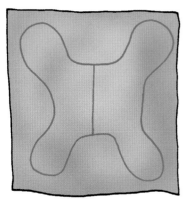

CUT FABRIC OR TISSUE PAPER TO FIT AND GLUE ONTO THE WING SHAPE; TAPE ON STRIPS OF FABRIC OR THICK RIBBONS FOR STRAPS

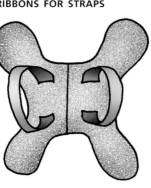

● Use the leftover bits of ribbon and a few extra flowers as decorations for a fairy wand. What else do you need?

● A fairy queen needs a throne! How would you turn a cardboard box or a pile of couch cushions into a royal seat?

The Complete Book of Flower Fairies by Cicely Mary Barker
Miss Rumphius by Barbara Cooney
The Gardener by Sarah Stewart
Thumbelina by Hans Christian Andersen

IMPROVISE!

If you don't have any strips of fabric at home, what else could you use for the "walls" of the fairy house?

Let's see, you have two wooden chairs and some old curtains. Can you arrange these items to make a smaller fairy house where you can still play inside? What if you also have a couple of old curtain rods — how would you use those as well?

DON'T FORGET A WREATH OF FLOWERS FOR YOUR HEAD!

A-Frame House

Can you guess why this house is called an A-frame? (Hint: look the outline of the roof.) Draw pictures of buildings or houses you know of that have peaked roofs like this. Then make one of your own!

Here's What You Need

✔ Large cardboard box
✔ Utility knife (for grownup use only)
✔ Tape

FINISHING TOUCHES
Paint and paintbrushes; child-safety scissors; construction paper; glue; paper-towel tubes; paper cups

MAKE YOUR A-FRAME HOUSE!

1. Place the box vertically, with the open end facing up. Here's how to make the roof:
Cut an A shape in the front and back of the box. Make sure the peak of the roof is below the top of the box so the sides meet when they are folded in. Fold in the sides of the box and tape the seams.

2. Cut out a few doors and windows.

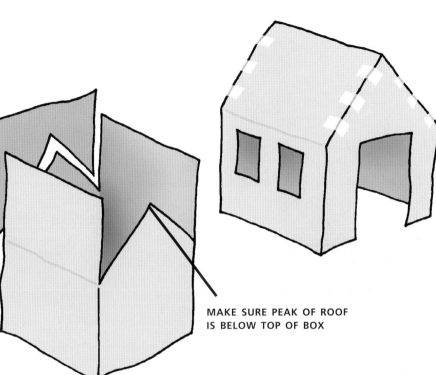

MAKE SURE PEAK OF ROOF
IS BELOW TOP OF BOX

CUT HOLE IN
PAPER CUP

FINISHING TOUCHES

Paint your house. Cut out and glue on construction-paper roof tiles.

Glue on rain gutters made from paper-towel tubes and paper cups. What happens when you put marbles in the gutters? Do you know what pulls them down?

MORE FUN!

- Paint the house to look like a gingerbread house. Cut candy shapes out of construction paper and glue them on. Now, act out the story of *Hansel and Gretel*!

- Make a CLOCK TOWER (see pages 42–43) and cut the bottom to fit the peak of your A-frame roof. Tape it in place. Now you've got a one-room schoolhouse!

- You can decorate this house in so many ways! How about a post office, a train station, or a doghouse? What others can you think of?

IMPROVISE!

Set up a small stepladder to make the A-frame shape. How could you use big pieces of cardboard to make the walls? What if you only have an old sheet?

Hansel and Gretel by Rika Lesser
Gingerbread Baby by Jan Brett

CHALLENGE LEVEL 1 2

This style of house is one you might see in the southwestern United States. The soil there has a lot of reddish clay in it, which makes a very sturdy brick called *adobe* (the Spanish word for clay). Go from room to room in your own adobe house!

Here's What You Need

✔ 2 medium cardboard boxes
✔ Large cardboard box
✔ Utility knife (for grownup use only)
✔ Tape

FINISHING TOUCHES
Paintbrush; watered-down glue; sand; glue; 2 wrapping-paper tubes; paper-towel tubes

Adobe House

MAKE YOUR ADOBE HOUSE!

1. Set up the medium boxes as shown, and trace around them onto the large box. Remove them to cut openings in the large box, then tape the boxes together.

CUT HOLE THROUGH THE ROOF BETWEEN THESE TWO BOXES

CUT DOOR HERE BETWEEN THESE TWO BOXES

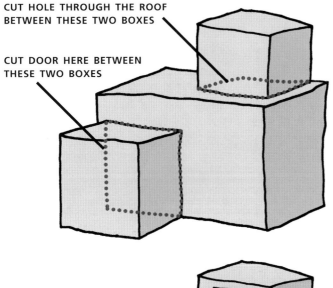

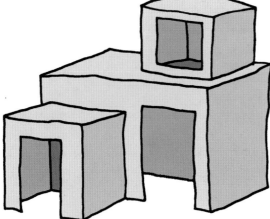

2. Cut out doors and windows.

FINISHING TOUCHES

Want your house to feel like real adobe bricks? Paint the house with the watered-down glue and sprinkle sand over it.

Traditional adobe houses have wooden ladders that reach to the upper levels. Can you make a pretend ladder by gluing together two empty wrapping-paper tubes and some paper-towel tubes?

MORE  FUN!

● Add more boxes for a larger house. What different room arrangements can you create?

● For some outside building fun, make abode bricks by mixing four parts of fine mud or clay with one part sand. Mix in water and some straw. Mold it in shoe boxes or cardboard juice cartons and let the sun bake the bricks until they are completely dry and hard. What can you build?

Shhh!

Little Hands Story Corner™

Arrow to the Sun: A Pueblo Indian Tale
  by Gerald McDermott
This House Is Made of Mud: Esta casa está hecha de lodo
  by Ken Buchanan

Nesting Houses

CHALLENGE LEVEL 1 2

Think of some everyday objects that nest inside each other. What about mixing bowls, coffee tables, or dolls? Now, how about houses that nest together in the same way?

Here's What You Need

✔ 3 large cardboard boxes (different sizes that fit inside each other)
✔ Utility knife (for grownup use only)

FINISHING TOUCHES
Paint and paintbrushes

MAKE YOUR NESTING HOUSES!

1. Place each box with the open end facing down. Cut out doors and windows.

FINISHING TOUCHES

Decorate with a theme. Create the houses from the nursery tale *The Three Little Pigs* by decorating the outside of one house to look like straw, another like sticks, and the third one like bricks. Or, how about Little Red Riding Hood's house and her grandmother's house. Decorate the third box to look like a forest. Now, act out the stories! What costumes will you need?

See COZY CARDBOARD HOUSE (pages 12–14) for more decorating ideas.

The Magic Nesting Doll by Jacqueline K. Ogburn
The Three Pigs by David Wiesner

Not by the hair of my chinny, chin, chin!

"R•O•O•M•Y" Cardboard House

CHALLENGE LEVEL 1 2

You can make this house any shape you like and with as many rooms as you like!

 Here's What You Need

✔ Large sheets of cardboard or large cardboard boxes, cut into panels
✔ Utility knife (for grownup use only)

FINISHING TOUCHES
Paint and paintbrushes; markers; construction paper; tape

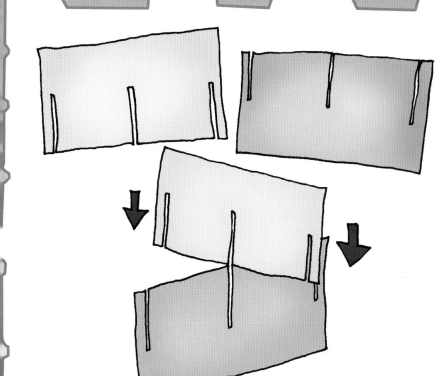

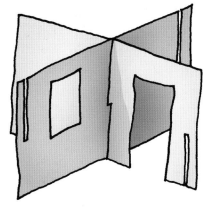

MAKE YOUR ROOMY HOUSE!

1. Cut slits in the cardboard sheets or panels from the edge to the center.

2. Make walls by connecting the cardboard pieces as shown.

3. Cut windows and doors.

FINISHING TOUCHES

Paint and decorate. How about some funny artwork to hang on the walls?

MORE FUN!

● See COZY CARDBOARD HOUSE (pages 12–14) for more decorating ideas.

● Make a maze and have a friend try it out! Pretend to be lost in your maze — can anyone find you? How about a haunted house maze — how would you decorate?

The Great, Big, Enormous, Gigantic Cardboard Box
  by Leeanne Brook

"ICY" IGLOO

✔ Hot-glue gun (for grownup use only)
✔ Clean plastic milk jugs

FINISHING TOUCHES
Sleeping bag; small sticks

CHALLENGE LEVEL 1 2

Start collecting empty milk jugs for blocks of "ice" and soon you'll have an igloo — with just enough room inside for you and a friend or two!

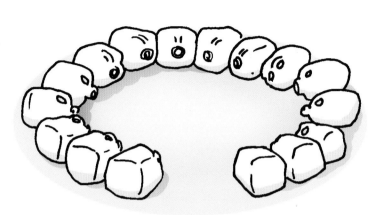

An *igloo*, built from blocks of ice, was the traditional winter home for the Inuit, who live in a very cold climate. Who are the Inuit people? Where do they live? How did they make summer homes?

MAKE YOUR ICY IGLOO!

1. Glue the milk jugs in a semicircle that's large enough for two to three children to fit inside. Leave space for a doorway.

2. Glue a second layer of milk jugs on top of the first layer, set in slightly.

3. Continue building up the walls, making each circle slightly smaller than the previous one. (The igloo will have a small opening at the top.)

FINISHING TOUCHES

Arrange your sleeping bag inside the igloo. How about a few sticks to make a pretend fire so you can cook your food?

Little Hands Story Corner™

Houses of Snow, Skin and Bones by Bonnie Shemie

Northern Lights: the Soccer Trails
  by Michael Arvaarluk Kusugak

Naya, the Inuit Cinderella by Brittany Marceau-Chenkie

MORE FUN!

● Walk on your knees — a traditional activity for Inuit kids. Kneel down on the grass or ground. Lift your heels toward the backs of your legs as you reach around and grab your feet from behind. Can you move?

IMPROVISE!

Try making the igloo out of other materials such as large pieces of plastic-foam packaging. Or, if you live in a cold climate, see if you can make one out of snow!

Newspaper-Roll Hut

CHALLENGE LEVEL 1 2 3

What is a hut? Where would you find one? The sides of a real hut are usually made with thick sticks or small trees, but newspaper rolls are an easy way to make sturdy walls for a play hut!

Here's What You Need

✔ Utility knife (for grownup use only)
✔ Large cardboard box
✔ Old newspapers
✔ Tape
✔ Rubber band

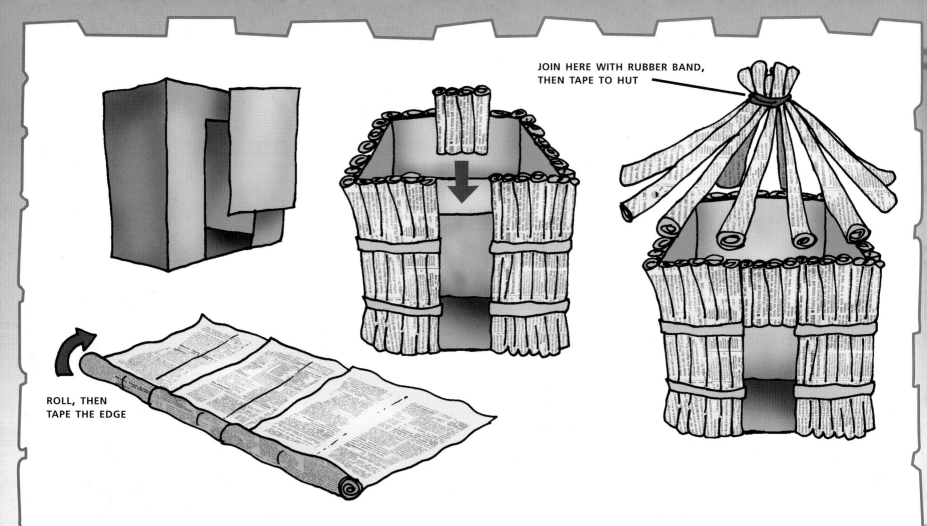

JOIN HERE WITH RUBBER BAND, THEN TAPE TO HUT

ROLL, THEN TAPE THE EDGE

MAKE YOUR NEWSPAPER-ROLL HUT!

1. Place the box vertically, open end facing up. Cut a door in one side.

2. Roll sections of newspaper into long tubes and tape securely.

3. Tape the rolls all around the outside of the cardboard box.

4. To make the roof, put 10 or more long rolls together and join them at one end with the rubber band. Place the roof on the hut and tape the ends of the newspaper rolls to the top of the hut.

MORE FUN!

● Paint your hut to look as if it's made of sticks. How about a thatched roof made of straw? What colors would you use?

● Make a village of huts. Link them together with a newspaper-roll fence as shown above.

Elsina's Clouds by Jeanette Winter
Who's in Rabbit's House: A Masai Tale
 by Verna Aardema
Gugu's House by Catherine Stock
Houses and Homes by Ann Morris

IMPROVISE!

If you don't have a big box, how could you arrange three chairs so they hold up the hut walls instead? If you're running short on newspaper, but you have a big piece of brown cloth, can you still make a roof?

Use the inside of a clean closet for your hut. How would you use newspaper rolls to make an entrance?

Come Right In!
Favorite Buildings & Structures

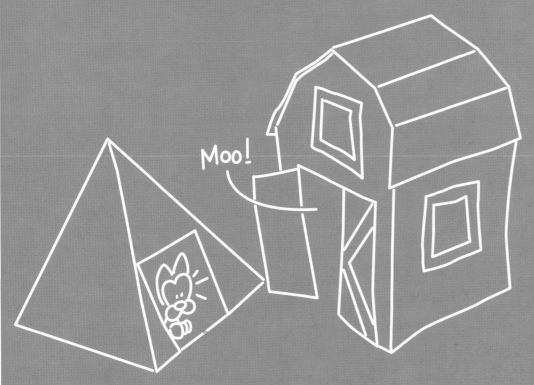

Moo!

Wouldn't it be fun to build a castle in the corner so you could pretend to be a knight or a princess? How about a big red barn where you can care for all your favorite stuffed animals? Or travel halfway around the world and build an Egyptian pyramid!

Here's a collection of fun-to-create play spaces that will take you on imaginary adventures near and far!

LITTLE Red Barn

CHALLENGE LEVEL 1 2

Do you have some stuffed animals that would like to live in a barn? Make one for them!

 ### Here's What You Need

✔ Large cardboard box
✔ Utility knife and scissors (for grownup use only)
✔ Tape
✔ Poster board, 2 to 3 sheets

FINISHING TOUCHES

Paint and paintbrushes; aluminum foil; tape; tall cardboard box; 2 sheets of poster board

 ### Learn More About It!

Is there a barn nearby that you could visit? Draw pictures of a barn or of life on a farm.

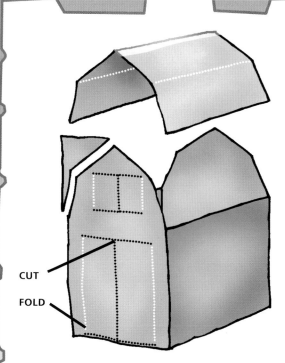

CUT

FOLD

MAKE YOUR LITTLE RED BARN!

1. Place the box horizontally, open end up. Cut an arch at the front and the back of the box as shown. Cut large double doors in the front as shown.

2. Tape the sheets of poster board together and tape them in place for the roof. Make it large enough to overhang the sides.

FINISHING TOUCHES

Paint the barn. What color are most barns? Cover the roof in aluminum foil or paint it gray.

Make a silo! Set the tall cardboard box on end and cut off the top and bottom flaps. Make the roof from two sheets of poster board overlapped and taped together. Cut the bottom edge as shown and tape the roof to the box.

SCORE (CUT HALFWAY THROUGH THE CARDBOARD) VERTICAL LINES DOWN THE CENTER OF EACH SIDE

FOLD ALONG THE SCORED LINES TO FORM AN OCTAGON

MORE  FUN!

● Fill the barn with hay. Hide plastic eggs in the hay and collect them in a basket.

● Sing "Old McDonald Had A Farm" and "The Farmer in the Dell."

And on this farm he had a very handsome cow...

 IMPROVISE!

Build the barn and silo out of large building blocks.

Turn a small table upside down. Use cardboard or pieces of old fabric to make the four sides of the barn. How could you use two hula hoops or foam swim noodles and an old sheet to make the rounded roof?

 Little Hands Story Corner™

Click, Clack, Moo: Cows that Type by Doreen Cronin
Big Red Barn Board Book by Margaret Wise Brown
Wake Up, Big Barn by Suzanne Chitwood

BIG STONE CASTLE

CHALLENGE LEVEL 1 2

Make a castle fit for a king and queen!

Here's What You Need

- ✔ Large cardboard box
- ✔ Utility knife (for grownup use only)
- ✔ Child-safety scissors
- ✔ Construction paper
- ✔ Tape

FINISHING TOUCHES
Paint and paintbrushes; blue sheet; construction paper; 4 thin dowels or pencils

MAKE YOUR BIG STONE CASTLE!

1. Place the box with the opening facing up. Cut along the top edges as shown. Cut out windows.

2. To make the drawbridge, cut out an arched doorway, leaving the bottom attached. Make two paper chains from construction-paper strips and tape them in place as shown.

FINISHING TOUCHES

Paint the castle walls in a pattern to look like stones. Place the blue sheet under the castle as a moat. Make flags out of construction paper; tape them to dowels or pencils and fly them from the corners.

MORE  FUN!

- Add more rooms to your castle with other boxes. Cut doors between them.

- Cut a medieval shield from cardboard. Decorate with paint.

- For a princess hat, roll stiff paper into a cone shape and tape. Trim the bottom as shown. Decorate with ribbons.

- For a crown, cut the edge of a narrow strip of paper as shown, then tape the ends together. Decorate with markers, stickers, and glitter.

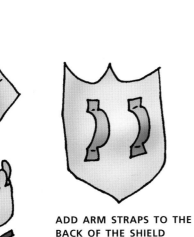

ADD ARM STRAPS TO THE
BACK OF THE SHIELD

Castle by David Macaulay
Knights and Castles by Will and Ma Osborne

CLOCK TOWER

Tick tock! What time is it? Time to play in the clock tower!

Here's What You Need

✔ 2 large cardboard boxes that are the same size
✔ Utility knife and scissors (for grownup use only)
✔ Tape
✔ Poster board
✔ Metal fastener

FINISHING TOUCHES

Paint and paintbrushes; construction paper; child-safety scissors; glue

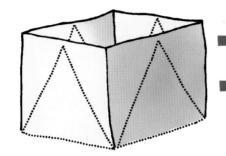

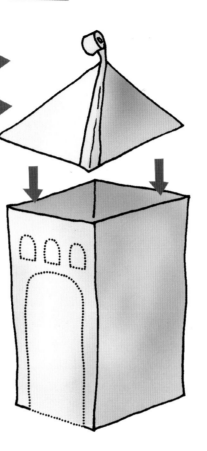

MAKE YOUR CLOCK TOWER!

1. Place one box with the open end facing up. Cut a large cardboard triangle out of each side as shown. Tape all the edges together to form a pyramid.

2. Place the second box vertically with the open end facing up. Tape the pyramid to the top of the box. Cut out a door and window.

3. Make a clock face and hands out of poster board. Attach to the box with a metal fastener.

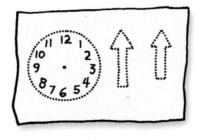

FINISHING TOUCHES

Paint the box to look like a stone tower. How about some ivy growing up the sides? Add some construction-paper roof tiles.

● What time is it? Show that time on the clock. What time do you go to bed? Change the clock hands to show that time.

● Act out the story of *Cinderella*.

Rapunzel by Paul O. Zelinsky
Clocks and More Clocks by Pat Hutchins

POINTED PYRAMID

How many sides does a triangle have? Use large cardboard triangles to make a four-sided structure called a *pyramid*. Thousands of years ago, the Egyptians built huge stone pyramids for the very powerful rulers of the time, called *pharaohs* (FA-rows). Some of these pyramids still stand today!

Here's What You Need

✔ 2 large cardboard boxes
✔ Tape
✔ Utility knife (for grownup use only)

FINISHING TOUCHES
Paint or watered-down glue and sand; paintbrush

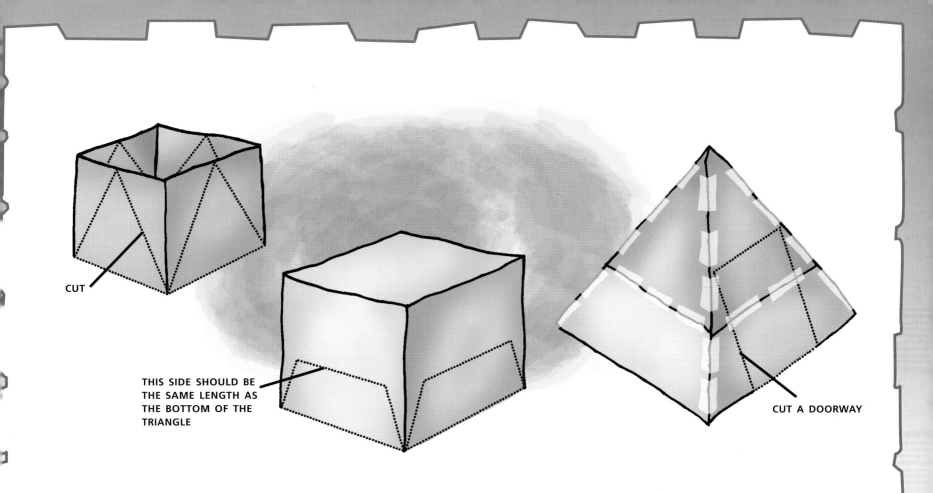

CUT

THIS SIDE SHOULD BE
THE SAME LENGTH AS
THE BOTTOM OF THE
TRIANGLE

CUT A DOORWAY

MAKE YOUR POINTED PYRAMID!

1. Place the box with the open end facing up. Cut a triangle out of each side as shown, making the triangles as large as possible. Tape them together to form a pyramid.

2. To make the pyramid taller, cut out four more cardboard shapes as shown. The top edge should be the same length as the bottom of the triangle. Tape the base together.

3. Place the pyramid on top of the base and tape them together. Cut a doorway.

FINISHING TOUCHES

Paint the pyramid yellow or orange to look like sand. Or, brush watered-down glue on the cardboard and sprinkle on sand (work on one section at a time).

Learn More About It!

Look at pictures of ancient pyramids in Egypt. It took thousands and thousands of stone blocks to make each one. The Great Pyramid (the largest one of all) is so big, it can be seen from the moon! Any ideas how these huge stone structures might have been built?

MORE FUN!

● Add a throne! The ancient Egyptians were the first people to put arms on chairs and use them as thrones for their kings and queens. Put an armchair near your pyramid and decorate it like a royal throne.

● Crown yourself pharaoh with an Egyptian-style crown. Wrap a piece of waxed paper around your head several times and tape it to stand tall. Shape the top into a small knob and tape to hold. Decorate with feathers and a construction-paper sun (signs of power).

Ms. Frizzle's Adventures: Ancient Egypt by Joanna Cole
Mummies, Pyramids and Pharaohs by Gail Gibbons
Pyramid by David Macaulay
Pyramids! 50 Hands-On Activities to Experience Ancient Egypt
   by Avery Hart & Paul Mantell

Who Lives Here?
Animal Homes & Habitats

Animals create all sorts of spaces for their homes, each one perfectly suited to that animal's needs. Try making your own versions of lots of different animal homes.

You'll see that when it comes to designing and building, our animal friends are superstars! And whether you like to pretend you're a wiggling worm or a busy beaver, you'll find these animal homes and habitats are great places to play!

Spider Web

Spiders spin sticky webs to catch their tasty meals of flies and other insects. Can you and your friends go from one side of this big spider web to the other without touching it? Oops! If you touch the string, you're "stuck" just like a fly! Who's the last fly left buzzing around?

Here's What You Need

✔ Chairs
✔ String

FINISHING TOUCHES
Child-safety scissors and stiff black paper or legs from old pantyhose and old newspaper; tape

Note to adults: When children use string, supervise them closely at all times.

MAKE YOUR SPIDER WEB!

1. Arrange the chairs in a circle. Use the string to weave a knee-high web between them.

FINISHING TOUCHES

Make a spider costume to wear! You have two arms and two legs — how many more do you need to be a spider? Cut them out of stiff paper or stuff pantyhose legs; attach them to your back.

● Sing "The Itsy-Bitsy Spider" as you act out the finger play. "I Know an Old Lady (Who Swallowed a Fly)" would be a fun song too!

Can you find a real spider's web? Look on fences, in bushes, and in blades of grass. With a grownup's help, use a spray bottle with a fine spray to mist the web gently with water so you can see the threads more clearly. Take a close look but don't disturb it!

The Very Busy Spider by Eric Carle
Spiders by Gail Gibbons
Anansi the Spider: A Tale from the Ashanti
   by Gerald McDermott
Spider's Lunch: All About Garden Spiders by Joanna Cole

CHALLENGE LEVEL 1

Can you wiggle like a worm through your very own tunnel?

Here's What You Need

✔ Rope
✔ 3 hula hoops
✔ Tape
✔ Chairs or other furniture
✔ Old sheet

Wiggly-Worm Tunnel

Note to adults: When children use rope, supervise them closely at all times.

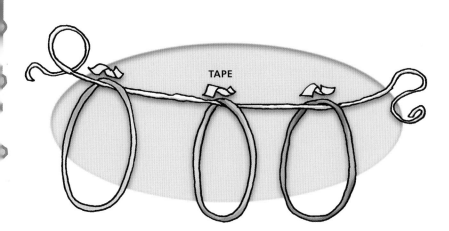

TAPE

MAKE YOUR WIGGLY-WORM TUNNEL!

1. Put the rope through the hula hoops. Tape the hoops to the rope about 3′ to 4′ (1 to 1.5 m) apart.

2. Attach the rope securely at two ends (tie each end to a piece of furniture, for example). The hula hoops should just touch the ground.

3. Drape the sheet over the hoops. Leave both ends of the tunnel open.

Learn More About It!

Worms have no arms or legs — how do they dig their way through the soil? Find out about some other tunnel-digging animals, like the star-nosed mole or a gopher.

MORE  FUN!

● Add more hoops to make the tunnel longer.

● Create the tunnel outdoors, using two trees.

● See if you can wiggle forward like a earthworm (don't use your hands or legs). An inchworm moves along by pushing up its middle section and then sliding its front end forward. Now give that a try!

Diary of a Worm by Doreen Cronin
Animal Architects: How Animals Weave, Tunnel, and Build Their Remarkable Homes by Wanda Shipman
Inch by Inch by Leo Lionni

CHALLENGE LEVEL 1 2 3

This cozy home can suit so many creatures. Crawl in and pretend to be a mouse, a mole, a rabbit, a fox, even a great big bear — anything that likes a underground den!

Here's What You Need

✔ Large cardboard box
✔ Utility knife (for grownup use only)
✔ Old newspaper
✔ Tape

FINISHING TOUCHES

Brown paint and paintbrush; glue, soil, leaves, and sticks; blankets and pillows

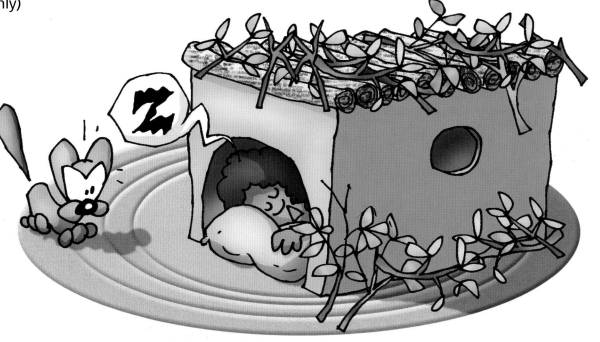

Underground BURROW

MAKE YOUR UNDERGROUND BURROW!

1. Place the box with the open end down. Cut an arched entrance and a window or two.

2. Roll and tape newspaper sections as shown on page 32. Cover the roof with the rolls; tape in place.

FINISHING TOUCHES

Paint the roof brown. Decorate the sides and roof of the house with the soil, leaves, and sticks. Inside, arrange the blankets and pillows to make a cozy nest.

 **Little Hands Story Corner**™

Miss Mouse's House
   by David Fleming
A New House For Mouse
   by Petr Horacek
Foxes and Their Homes
   by Deborah Chase Gibson
No Place Like Home
   by Jonathan Emmett
Time to Sleep
   by Denise Fleming

 **MORE FUN!**

● Tape construction-paper mouse ears or rabbit ears to a headband. Put on your "ears," curl up in your burrow, and snack on some cheese or munch some carrots. How would you pretend to be a fox or a mole? How about a hibernating bear?

 **IMPROVISE!**

Place two chairs back to back. What could you drape over the top to create a space where you could curl up inside? How about a big soft armchair and an old sheet — can you make a burrow out of that?

Use some big soft pillows to turn a closet into a cozy animal den!

Bird's Nest

Build a cozy nest from newspaper "twigs" that's just big enough for you and a friend!

Here's What You Need

✔ Old newspaper
✔ Tape

FINISHING TOUCHES
Brown paint and paintbrush; leaves and dried grasses or construction paper and child-safety scissors; glue; string or yarn; blankets and pillows

MAKE YOUR BIRD'S NEST!

1. Roll and tape the newspaper sections as shown on page 32. Make about 20 rolls to start; you may need more.

2. Arrange a layer of newspaper twigs in a large circle on the floor. Tape them together. Continue taping newspaper rolls in place to make the sides as high as you like.

FINISHING TOUCHES

Paint the twigs. Add some leaves and grass (real or construction paper). How about weaving in a bit of string or yarn? What other materials might a bird use to make a nest? Arrange the blankets and pillows and settle into your cozy nest!

 **Learn More About It!**

Can you find a real bird's nest outdoors? Ask an adult friend to help you use a field guide to figure out what kind of bird lives in it. Draw a picture of your feathered neighbor.

Put a bird feeder up outside. What kinds of birds come to visit? What do they like to eat?

MORE  FUN!

● Fill your nest with baby birds (invite a few friends to play with you or use stuffed animals). Pretend to gather food for them. How would you teach them to fly? Now you take a turn being the baby bird trying its wings for the first time!

IMPROVISE!

Build the nest shape out of big cardboard building blocks; then cover it with an old blanket. How about using an small plastic or inflatable swimming pool? Can you make a nest if you only have big pillows to use?

Try making your nest outside. Pound several stakes into the ground or arrange branches to form a circle. Weave strips of cloth between them. If you don't have any cloth, what natural materials could you find outdoors to use?

Little Hands Story Corner™

The Wonderful House by Margaret Wise Brown
Are You My Mother? by P. D. Eastman
A House Is a House for Me by Mary Ann Hoberman

CHALLENGE LEVEL 1 2 3

Beavers have very sharp front teeth (they can gnaw down entire trees!), and they are strong swimmers. They use small trees, sticks, and mud to make a house called a *lodge* in the middle of a pond. Get "busy as a beaver" and make your own lodge from newspaper rolls.

Here's What You Need

✔ Large cardboard box
✔ Utility knife (for grownup use only)
✔ Old newspaper
✔ Tape

FINISHING TOUCHES
Brown paint and paintbrush; twigs and leaves or construction paper and child-safety scissors; glue

BEAVER LODGE

MAKE YOUR BEAVER LODGE!

1. Place the box open side down. In one side, cut a small entrance as shown.

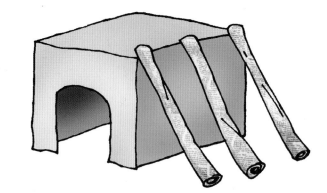

2. Roll the newspaper sections and tape them as shown on page 32. Make at least 20 rolls to start; you might need more.

3. Place three rolls from the floor up to the top of the box as shown. Tape them in place. Tape other rolls horizontally across the first three.

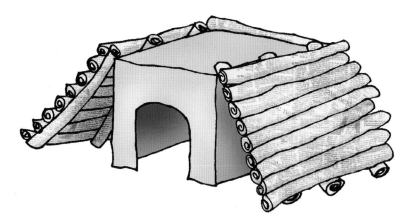

4. Repeat step 3 on two more sides of the box, leaving the doorway open. Cover the top with more rolls. Add as many more log rolls as you like to give it the look of a real beaver lodge!

FINISHING TOUCHES

Paint the logs brown. Weave in twigs and leaves from outdoors or glue on paper ones.

MORE  FUN!

● Beavers have broad, flat tails. They use them to steer while they're swimming and when they sense danger, they slap their tails loudly on the water as a warning. How could you make a pretend beaver tail?

● Use big cardboard blocks to raise the lodge up so you can "swim" up into it like a real beaver. Or, if you have twin beds at home, try setting the lodge on the beds so it rests between them. What else could you use to raise the box up?

IMPROVISE!

How could you make the lodge without the cardboard box? Could you use a small table or a few chairs arranged back to back to hold up the rolls?

Try building an outdoor beaver lodge up against a fence using sticks and mud.

Learn More About It!

Look at a picture of a real beaver lodge. The beavers have to dive underwater to go in the front door! What do you think they do all winter while the pond is frozen?

Beaver at Long Pond by William T. George and Lindsay Barrett George
Building Beavers by Kathleen Martin-James
Whose House? by Barbara Seuling

FOREST LOG

FINISHING TOUCHES
Paint and paintbrush; moss, bark, and leaves or construction paper and child-safety scissors; glue; blanket

CHALLENGE LEVEL 1 2 3

A fallen log is crawling with life! All kinds of creatures travel over, under, and even through it. Which one will you be?

Here's What You Need

✔ Chicken wire and wire cutters (for grownup use only)
✔ Cardboard
✔ Tape
✔ *Papier-mâché supplies:* Bowl; spoon; measuring cup; flour; water; old newspaper

MAKE YOUR FOREST LOG!

1. Make a large roll out of the chicken wire (large enough to crawl through). Fold over any cut metal edges to secure them. Cover all sharp points thoroughly with cardboard, taping it securely in place.

2. *Prepare the papier-mâché:* In the bowl, mix one part flour to three parts water to make a smooth paste. Tear several sections of the newspaper into strips.

3. Cover the floor with old newspaper. Working on a section of the outside of the log at a time, dip the newspaper strips into the paste and use them to thoroughly cover the chicken wire. Let dry completely. Cover the top with a second layer; let dry.

FINISHING TOUCHES

Paint the log. Decorate it with moss, bark, and leaves (real or construction paper). Spread out the blanket inside.

● Make bugs out of clothespins, fabric scraps, pipe cleaners, and construction paper. Stick them all over the log and inside it, too. How about a few hanging from the ceiling?

PIPE-CLEANER AND
BLACK-WALNUT BUG

PIPE-CLEANER,
PAPER, AND CLOTHESPIN
BUTTERFLY

A Tree Is Nice by Janice May Udry
A Log's Life by Wendy Pfeffer
Once Upon a Lily Pad: Froggy Love in Monet's Garden by Joan Sweeney
In the Small, Small Pond by Denise Fleming

Anthill

Ants are busy creatures, scurrying in and out of their nests, where they dig tunnels and store food. Create your own anthill, complete with a cozy nest inside!

 ## Here's What You Need

✔ Large cardboard box
✔ Utility knife (for grownup use only)
✔ Old newspaper
✔ Tape
✔ *Papier-mâché supplies:* Bowl; spoon; measuring cup; flour; water; old newspaper

FINISHING TOUCHES
Brown paint and paintbrush; glue; leaves, sand or soil, and grass or construction paper and child-safety scissors

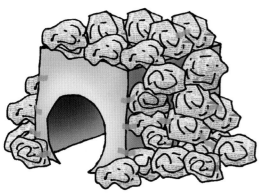

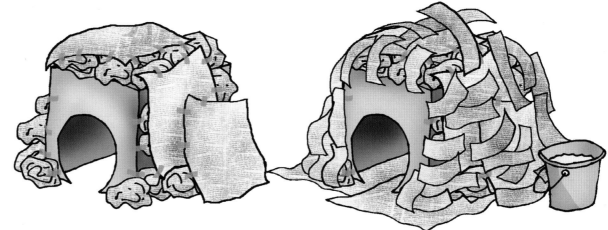

MAKE YOUR ANTHILL!

1. Place the box open end facing down. Cut a hole for an entrance.

2. Place crumpled newspaper all around and on top of the box. Tape in place.

3. Tape flat sheets of newspaper all over the anthill for a smooth finish.

4. *Prepare the papier-mâché:* In the bowl, mix one part flour to three parts water and stir to make a smooth paste. Tear several sections of the newspaper into strips.

5. Protect the floor with old newspaper. Dip the strips of newspaper into papier-mâché mixture and use them to cover the anthill. Let dry completely. Cover with a second layer; let dry.

FINISHING TOUCHES

Paint the anthill brown. Decorate the outside with leaves, sand or soil, and grass. Or, create some colorful leaves from big sheets of construction paper. Before you cut, imagine you're an ant — how big would each leaf look to you?

MORE FUN!

- Crawl inside and sing "The Ants Go Marching."

- An underground ant nest can be quite large, with tunnels that lead to "rooms" where ants store their food. Add additional rooms to your anthill and connect them with box tunnels.

- Some types of ants mound soil to make a nest on top of the ground — some reaching a foot or two (30 to 60 cm) in height! How high can you make your anthill?

I can't find my room.

Learn More About It!

Make an ant farm in a clear container (a bottle, a large jar, or empty fish tank, for example). With a grownup's help, fill it with sand or soil and add some garden ants. Cover the top with a nylon stocking and secure it with a rubber band. Wrap the container in black paper. Peek under the paper occasionally to see the tunnels that the ants form. To feed them, place tiny bits of fruit and a dab of jam or honey on the soil surface; a moist cotton ball will provide them with water.

Little Hands Story Corner™

Roberto, the Insect Architect
   by Nina Laden
Ant Cities by Arthur Dorros
Are You an Ant? by Judy Allen

Let's Get Moving!
All Kinds of Things that Go

Aarr!

Do you like to zoom along on wheels, paddle on water, or soar into the air? Here you can do all three! Go down in your submarine, pick up passengers in your taxi, or take the controls of your very own front-end loader!

Whether you dream of being a firefighter, a pirate, or an astronaut, you'll have lots of imaginary adventures making things that roll, float, and fly.

Tricycle Taxi

Need to get somewhere quickly? Call a cab! Take turns with a friend being the taxi driver or the passenger.

CHALLENGE LEVEL 1

Here's What You Need

✔ Rope and scissors (for grownup use only)
✔ Plastic laundry basket or wagon
✔ Tricycle

FINISHING TOUCHES
Glue; red, yellow, and green construction paper; child-safety scissors; shoe box; string; poster board or stiff paper; markers; tape; chairs

MAKE YOUR TRICYCLE TAXI!

1. Tie the laundry basket or the wagon to the back of the tricycle so that no more than 6" (15 cm) of string is between them. (As the taxi driver pedals along, be careful that the basket doesn't bang into the tricycle.)

FINISHING TOUCHES

Glue red, yellow, and green paper circles on the shoe box to make a traffic signal. Hang the light from the ceiling. Make traffic signs out of poster board or stiff paper; tape them to chairs.

MORE FUN!

● Take your stuffed animals for a ride. Drop them off at their destinations!

● Play Red Light, Green Light.

● You have to pay money to ride in a taxi. Make some construction-paper dollars. Attach a small box to the handlebars to collect the money from your passengers, called the *fare*.

The Adventures of Taxi Dog by Debra and Sal Barracca
Taxi Driver! Dashing around New York City by Robyn Brode

BATHTUB SUBMARINE

You don't need water to have hours of fun in this submarine!

Here's What You Need

✔ Medium cardboard box
✔ Utility knife and scissors (for grownup use only)
✔ Bathtub
✔ Tape

FINISHING TOUCHES
Bathtub crayons or bathtub paints and paintbrush; paper-towel tube; tape

Note to adults: When children play in or near water, supervise them closely at all times.

MAKE YOUR BATHTUB SUBMARINE!

1. In one side of the box, cut large round windows, called *portholes*. Place the box on the edges of the tub, open end down. Tape in place.

FINISHING TOUCHES

Use the bathtub crayons or paints to draw underwater scenes on the sides of the tub. (You can make your own bathtub paint by mixing tempera paint and shampoo and adding a little cornstarch to thicken it.)

Make a periscope out of the paper-towel tube. Tape it to the top of the box.

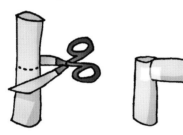

 **Learn More About It!**

Look at pictures of real submarines. What do you need to see above the water? How does a real periscope work?

Little Hands Story Corner™

Rub-a-Dub Sub by Linda Ashman
Submarine (Eyewitness Books) by Neil Mallard

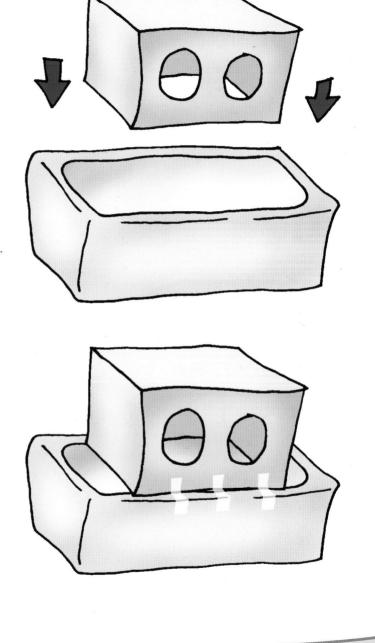

Draw a picture of your favorite kind of car. Now see if you can make a great big cardboard one that looks just like it!

Cruising Car

Here's What You Need

- ✔ Medium cardboard box
- ✔ Utility knife and scissors (for grownup use only)
- ✔ Disposable aluminum baking pan
- ✔ Tape
- ✔ 4–5 paper plates
- ✔ Red plastic cup
- ✔ 2–3 disposable aluminum pie plates
- ✔ Old pot lid with a round handle (optional)
- ✔ Metal fastener
- ✔ Cardboard tubes
- ✔ Clear plastic

FINISHING TOUCHES

Paint and paintbrush; cardboard scraps; paper cup; shoe box; aluminum foil; construction paper

MAKE YOUR CRUISING CAR!

1. Place the box horizontally, open side up. Cut down three of the sides as shown. In the remaining section, cut a hole for a windshield. Cut out a door.

2. Cut the aluminum baking pan as shown and tape all the sharp edges. Tape in place for a shiny front grille!

3. Add wheels, brake lights, headlights — and whatever else your car needs to really cruise!

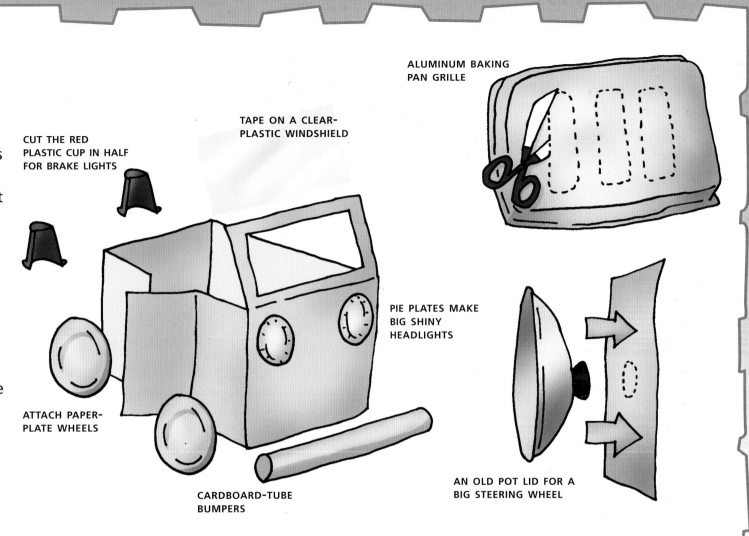

CUT THE RED PLASTIC CUP IN HALF FOR BRAKE LIGHTS

TAPE ON A CLEAR-PLASTIC WINDSHIELD

ALUMINUM BAKING PAN GRILLE

PIE PLATES MAKE BIG SHINY HEADLIGHTS

ATTACH PAPER-PLATE WHEELS

CARDBOARD-TUBE BUMPERS

AN OLD POT LID FOR A BIG STEERING WHEEL

4. For a steering wheel that turns, attach a paper or pie plate with a metal fastener. You can also use an old pot lid with a round handle. Trace around the handle on the front of the box and cut out the circle. Push the handle through the hole; it should fit snugly.

FINISHING TOUCHES

Paint your car! Make cardboard keys and an ignition switch (see page 102). Glue on a shoe-box glove compartment. Cut out cardboard mirrors and wrap them in aluminum foil; tape them in place. Don't forget a license plate! What could you use for a seat belt? How could you make a cup holder or a gas pedal? For a gearshift idea, see page 93.

- Take good care of your car! Put toy wrenches and a hammer in a cardboard six-pack carrier for a handy tool kit. The top of a plastic milk jug makes a good spout for pouring oil into a car.

- Make road signs out of cardboard and tape them to the backs of chairs. Cut a hole in the bottom of the box and attach ribbon suspenders so that you can "drive" around in your car.

- Don't run out of gas! Make a gas pump (see page 78).

- Turn your car into a taxi or a police car. Or, make it fly by adding wings or a propeller!

Little Red Car Plays Taxi by Mathew Price
Cars at Play by Rick Walton

So, what kind of mileage are you getting?

CHALLENGE LEVEL 1 2

Flash your flashlight and blast your whistle siren —
you're off to fight fires in your big fire truck!

Here's What You Need

✔ Medium or large cardboard box
✔ Utility knife and scissors (for grownup use only)
✔ 2 paper plates
✔ 4 disposable aluminum pie plates
✔ Red plastic cup
✔ Tape
✔ Clear plastic
✔ Extra cardboard (or save one of the box flaps)

FIRE ENGINE

FINISHING TOUCHES

Paint and paintbrush; paper plate;
piece of old garden hose; paper plate
or aluminum pie plate and metal fastener
or old pot lid; recycled items
for control-panel buttons, knobs,
and dials (bottle caps, empty film
canisters, cup bottoms, etc.); paper cup

MAKE YOUR FIRE ENGINE!

1. Place the box horizontally, open side up. Cut out a door and windshield as shown.

2. Now get your fire engine ready to race to the scene of a fire! See the illustration below for ideas.

3. For a ladder, cut the extra cardboard as shown. Attach it to the box.

FINISHING TOUCHES

Paint your fire engine. Why are fire engines always bright colors?

Cut a hole in the side of the fire engine and tape one end of the hose section in place.

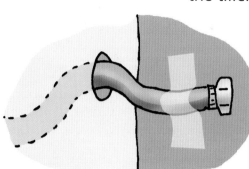

Add a steering wheel (see page 71). Some ladder trucks are so long, they need a second steering wheel, called the *tiller*, in the back! One firefighter (the *tillerman*) rides way at the back of the truck and steers the back end.

Add dials, buttons, and controls to your dashboard. To make an ignition switch, see page 102.

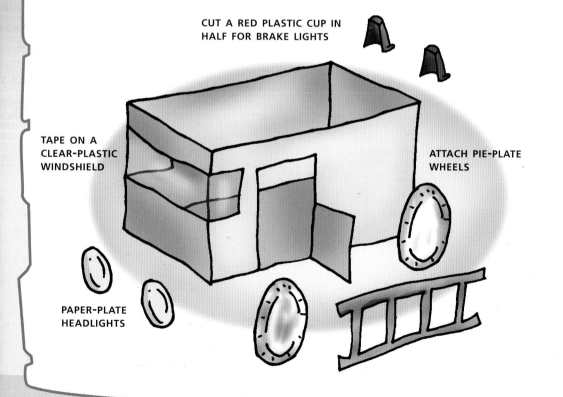

CUT A RED PLASTIC CUP IN HALF FOR BRAKE LIGHTS

TAPE ON A CLEAR-PLASTIC WINDSHIELD

ATTACH PIE-PLATE WHEELS

PAPER-PLATE HEADLIGHTS

MORE 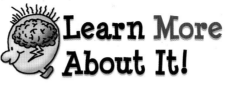 FUN!

● Dress up like a firefighter in a hat, boots, and a big jacket. Make an oxygen tank out of an empty cereal box. How could you attach it to your back?

● Make the A-FRAME HOUSE (see pages 18–20) and decorate it to look like a fire station, with a big overhead door in front. Add a rescue crew with a couple of cars (see CRUISING CAR, pages 70–72) decorated to look like a police car and an ambulance.

Learn More About It!

Ask a grownup to visit the local fire department with you. Or, meet a volunteer firefighter.

Even Firefighters Hug Their Moms
  by Christine Kole MacLean
A Fire Engine for Ruthie
  by Leslea Newman
Fire Truck by Peter Sis

Here's a handy truck for hauling big loads. What will you carry?

Here's What You Need

- ✔ 2 medium cardboard boxes
- ✔ Utility knife and scissors (for grownup use only)
- ✔ Tape
- ✔ Pipe cleaner
- ✔ Child-safety scissors
- ✔ Black construction paper
- ✔ Glue
- ✔ Paper plate
- ✔ Metal fastener
- ✔ Old pot lid with round handle (optional)

FINISHING TOUCHES

Paint and paintbrush; paper plates or disposable aluminum pie plates; construction paper; markers; bumper stickers; paper cup; shoe box; empty film canister or cap; disposable aluminum pan

DUMP TRUCK

CHALLENGE LEVEL 1 2

MAKE YOUR DUMP TRUCK!

1. Place the boxes with the open sides facing up. Use one box for the cab. Cut sections out of two sides as shown. Fold down the front and tape it as shown.

2. Attach the cab to the back of the truck with the pipe cleaner as shown.

3. Cut wheels out of the black construction paper as shown and glue them on. Attach the paper plate with a metal fastener to make a steering wheel. Or to use an old pot lid, see page 71.

FINISHING TOUCHES

Paint your truck. Add headlights. Add a construction-paper license plate. Decorate your truck with bumper stickers.

To add an ignition switch, see page 102. For dashboard ideas, see pages 72 and 74.

Glue on a shoe-box engine compartment. What could you glue inside the box to look like the parts of a real engine? Add a shiny grille on the front (see page 71).

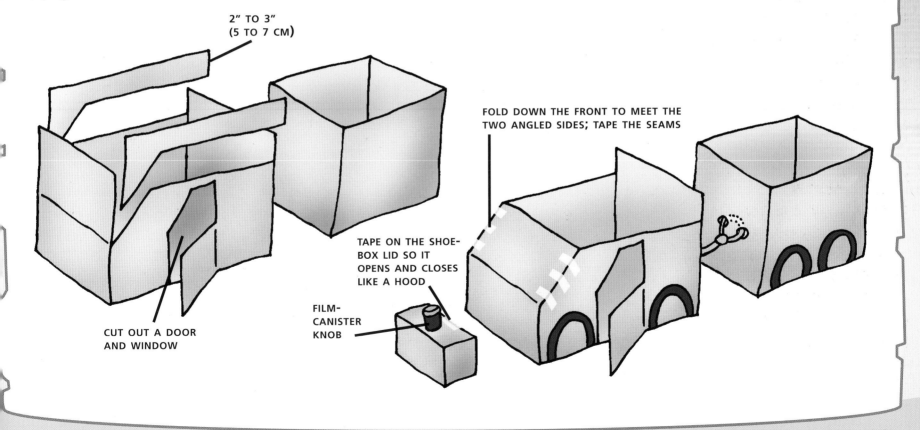

2" TO 3"
(5 TO 7 CM)

CUT OUT A DOOR AND WINDOW

FILM-CANISTER KNOB

TAPE ON THE SHOE-BOX LID SO IT OPENS AND CLOSES LIKE A HOOD

FOLD DOWN THE FRONT TO MEET THE TWO ANGLED SIDES; TAPE THE SEAMS

Learn More About It!

With a grownup friend, visit a construction site. From a safe distance, watch the vehicles and the heavy machinery at work.

● Make a gas pump out of an old plastic garbage can or a large box and a length of old garden hose.

Truck by Donald Crews
Get to Work Trucks! by Don Carter
Cars and Trucks and Things That Go
   by Richard Scarry

CUT A HOLE THE DIAMETER OF THE HOSE; TAPE IT IN PLACE

All aboard! Blow your whistle, collect the tickets and you're off!

Here's What You Need

- ✔ Large cardboard box
- ✔ Glue
- ✔ Small box
- ✔ Utility knife and scissors (for grownup use only)
- ✔ Cylindrical container (thick cardboard tube, coffee can, or oatmeal container)
- ✔ Tape
- ✔ White tissue paper
- ✔ Construction paper
- ✔ Cardboard tubes
- ✔ Shoe box

FINISHING TOUCHES
Construction paper; child-safety scissors; markers

Traveling Train

MAKE YOUR TRAVELING TRAIN!

1. Place the large box horizontally, open side up. Glue the small box to the front of it. If necessary, cut a windshield and windows so you can see out when you're sitting in the box.

2. Use the cylindrical container for a smokestack. Add wheels and a throttle.

FINISHING TOUCHES

Trains often have fancy names that make them sound fast, like The Flying Scotsman or the Hogwarts Express. Tape a sign with the name and number of your train on the side of the engine.

Make your train from a row of chairs. Give the engineer the biggest chair all the way up front! Can you still have wheels and a throttle? What other finishing touches could you add?

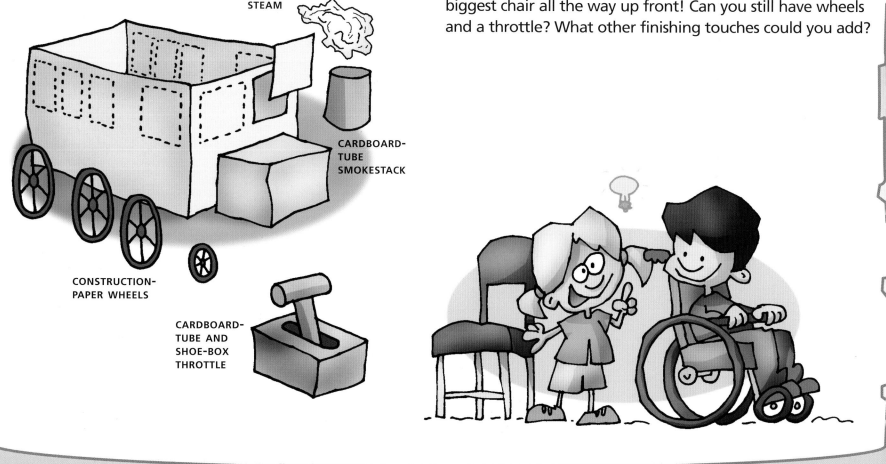

TISSUE-PAPER STEAM

CARDBOARD-TUBE SMOKESTACK

CONSTRUCTION-PAPER WHEELS

CARDBOARD-TUBE AND SHOE-BOX THROTTLE

MORE  FUN!

● Use more boxes to make cars for your train — passenger cars, a coal car, a box car to carry freight. Don't forget a little red caboose!

● Make tickets and have someone collect them. Where is your train headed? Tape tracks on the ground. Tape signs around the room with the names of the stops your train makes.

● Make a train station (see A-FRAME HOUSE, pages 18–20).

● Sing "I've Been Working On The Railroad," "Casey Jones," "Little Red Caboose," or "Engine, Engine, Number Nine" as you chug along!

Learn More About It!

With a grownup, visit a train station. Look at the train schedule and watch for a train to arrive at the station. Is it running on time?

Freight Train by Donald Crews
The Polar Express by Chris Van Allsburg
The Caboose Who Got Loose by Bill Peet
The Little Engine that Could by Watty Piper

High-Flying Helicopter

A whirlybird is a nickname for a helicopter! Can you see why? Make a helicopter with a propeller that really spins!

Here's What You Need

✔ Medium cardboard box
✔ Utility knife (for grownup use only)
✔ Pencil
✔ Wrapping-paper tube
✔ Tape

FINISHING TOUCHES

Shoe-box lid; aluminum foil; recycled items for control-panel buttons and knobs (bottle caps, empty film canisters, paper-cup bottoms, etc.); metal fasteners; paper cup; cardboard scraps

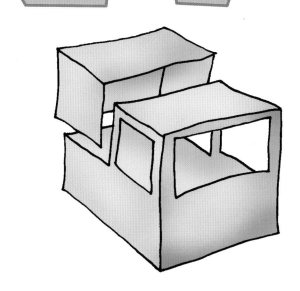

MAKE YOUR HIGH-FLYING HELICOPTER!

1. Place the box horizontally, open side down. Cut out a section as shown.

2. Cut out doors, windows, and a windshield. You might need a sunroof to fit comfortably inside.

3. From the extra cardboard, cut out two pieces for a propeller. Trace around the cardboard tube in the center of each blade and on the top of the box; cut out the circles. Assemble the propeller on the helicopter; tape the bottom in place to secure it.

FINISHING TOUCHES

Cover a shoe-box lid with aluminum foil and make a control panel for the dashboard (see pages 72 and 74 for ideas). Use metal fasteners to make things that spin. To make an ignition switch, see page 102. Cut keys from the cardboard scraps.

MORE FUN!

● Wear a colander helmet. How about a backpack for a parachute? What could you use for a seat belt?

● Check out the sights with a pair of cardboard-tube binoculars while you fly!

Budgie The Little Helicopter by Sarah Ferguson
The Flyers by Allan Drummond

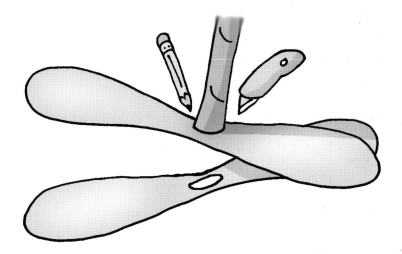

Pirate Ship

Shiver me timbers! Make this seaworthy pirate ship and set sail on the high seas!

Here's What You Need

- ✔ Large cardboard box with flaps
- ✔ Utility knife (for grownup use only)
- ✔ Tape
- ✔ Wooden pole or wrapping-paper tube
- ✔ Poster board

FINISHING TOUCHES

Paint and paintbrush; wrapping-paper tubes; extra cardboard; lid from an old pot (optional); scraps of construction paper or fabric; child safety scissors; glue

MAKE YOUR PIRATE SHIP!

1. Place the box horizontally, open side up, and cut off the flaps. Tape two of them on the box front to create a triangular-shaped bow as shown.

2. Attach a sail.

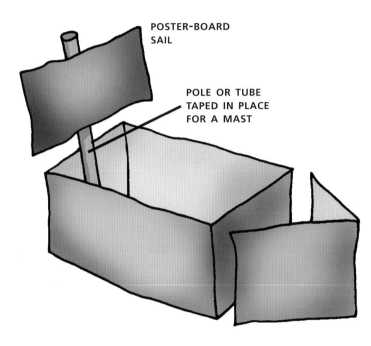

POSTER-BOARD SAIL

POLE OR TUBE TAPED IN PLACE FOR A MAST

FINISHING TOUCHES

Paint the ship. Make oars out of wrapping-paper tubes (or use brooms or hockey sticks). Add a steering wheel cut from cardboard or use the pot lid (see page 71).

Hoist a flag to the top of the mast! The pirate's flag, with a skull and crossbones, is called the Jolly Roger.

MORE FUN!

● Dress up like a pirate!

● Make an old treasure map on a crumpled piece of paper torn from a brown-paper grocery bag. Hunt for treasure!

How I Became a Pirate by Melinda Long
Edward and the Pirates by David McPhail
A Pirate's Life for Me by Julie Thompson and Brownie Macintosh

PAPER-TOWEL TUBE FOR A SPYGLASS

Rock on the waves as you cross the seas in your ocean-going ship!

Here's What You Need

✔ 2 large sheets of cardboard or large cardboard box
✔ Utility knife (for grownup use only)
✔ Broom or wooden pole
✔ Tape
✔ Construction paper
✔ Markers

FINISHING TOUCHES

Paint and paintbrush; shells; sand; glue; strip of cardboard; tape

Rocking Boat

MAKE YOUR ROCKING SHIP!

1. Cut two identical half-circles out of cardboard as shown. Cut windows in the sides of each.

2. Place the broom handle or pole between the two half-circles and tape the center seam. Make a construction-paper flag and tape it to the broom handle.

FINISHING TOUCHES

Paint wavy lines on the boat bottom for ocean waves. Add some green seaweed growing all over the boat. How about some sea treasures: seashells, a starfish, or barnacles? Glue on some sand and some real shells, too.

Paint the name of your boat on a strip of cardboard and tape it to the end of the boat (called the *stern*).

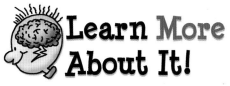 **Learn More About It!**

There are many different kinds of boats: motorboats, sailboats, barges, cruise ships, tugboats, canoes, kayaks, and rowboats. Draw pictures of the boats you know. What kinds of boats have you been in?

 **IMPROVISE!**

See if you can make your ship out of a rocking chair and two large pieces of cardboard or a big cardboard box.

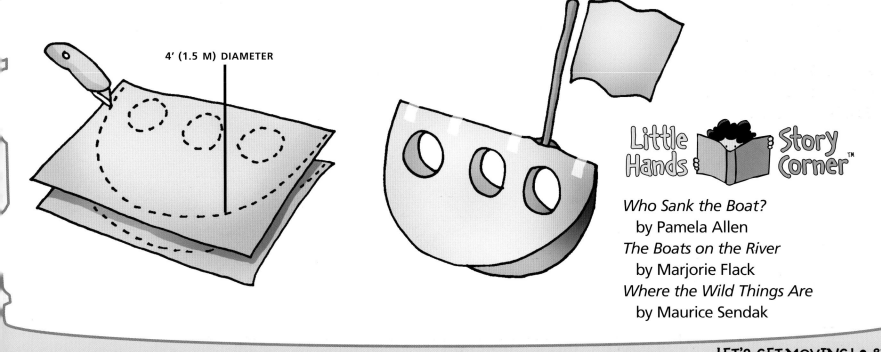

4' (1.5 M) DIAMETER

Little Hands Story Corner™

Who Sank the Boat?
 by Pamela Allen
The Boats on the River
 by Marjorie Flack
Where the Wild Things Are
 by Maurice Sendak

SOARING SPACESHIP

Get ready for countdown and head for outer space in your spaceship! What will you bring with you to the moon?

Here's What You Need

✔ Large cardboard box
✔ Utility knife and scissors (for grownup use only)
✔ Medium cardboard box
✔ Glue
✔ Stiff paper
✔ Tape
✔ Cylindrical container (thick cardboard tube, oatmeal container, coffee can)

FINISHING TOUCHES

Aluminum foil; paint and paintbrush; recycled items for control-panel buttons, knobs, and dials (bottle caps, empty film canisters, cup bottoms, etc.); 4 empty aluminum cans

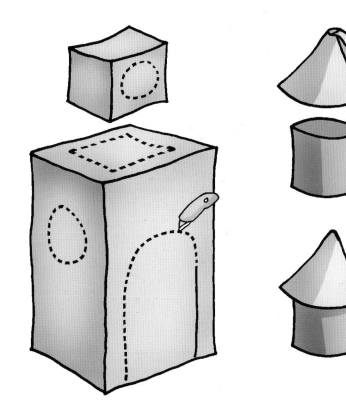

FINISHING TOUCHES

Decorate the ship with aluminum foil and paint. Paint the name of your mission on the outside.

Spaceships have lots of dials, buttons, and switches. See pages 72 and 74 for some control-panel ideas.

Tape the four aluminum cans (open end down so no sharp edges are exposed) in the bottom corners.

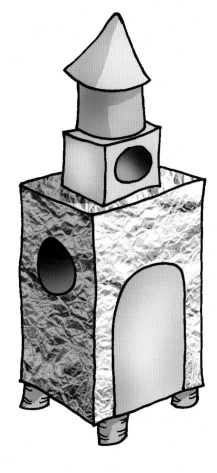

MAKE YOUR SPACESHIP!

1. Place the large box vertically, open end down. Cut out a door (called the *hatch*) and some round windows.

2. Cut a window in the medium box. Place it on top of the larger box and cut a hole between the boxes. Glue the boxes together.

3. Roll a cone out of the stiff paper and tape it to the top of the cylinder. Glue it on the very top of the spaceship.

Make a lunar landscape! Prick small holes in pieces of black paper and use them to cover the windows. Scatter soft items such as crumpled newspaper, bubble wrap, and small pillows on the ground and cover them with an old sheet. Are you ready to walk on the moon?

Roaring Rockets by Tony Mitton
I Want to be an Astronaut by Byron Barton
What Eddie Can Do by Wilfried Gebhard
The Moon Book by Gail Gibbons
And If the Moon Could Talk by Kate Banks

MORE FUN!

Dress up like astronauts! For a helmet, cut a plastic milk jug in half and cover it with aluminum foil. For space shoes, strap on big sponges with rubber bands. Attach a cereal-box oxygen tank with ribbon straps.

Objects float in outer space! Tape fishing line to objects and hang them inside the spaceship to simulate lack of gravity.

Eat like an astronaut. Try eating pudding from a ziplock plastic bag using a straw. Drink from juice boxes.

CHALLENGE LEVEL 1 2

What can you lift with this front-end loader? Make a dump truck (pages 76–77) to go with it and you're ready for a day of hard work at the construction site!

Here's What You Need

✔ Large cardboard box
✔ Utility knife (for grownup use only)
✔ Medium cardboard box
✔ 2 wrapping-paper tubes
✔ Tape
✔ Black paper

FINISHING TOUCHES

Paint and paintbrushes; recycled items for dashboard controls (bottle caps, empty film canisters; paper-cup bottoms, etc.); glue; 4 paper plates or construction paper, black marker; wrapping-paper tubes; plastic balls

Front-End Loader

MAKE YOUR FRONT-END LOADER!
1. Place the large box vertically, open end up. Cut a door in the side and a big window in the front. Cut the roof in an arch shape as shown.

2. Cut the medium box as shown to look like the bucket of a front-end loader. Attach it to the wrapping-paper tubes as shown.

3. Make an exhaust pipe by rolling black paper into a cylinder. Tape it to the cab.

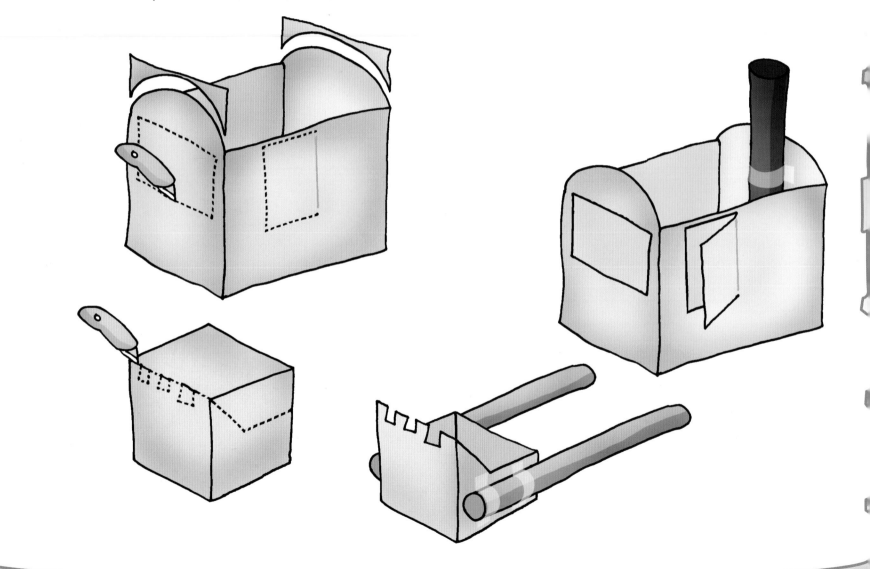

FINISHING TOUCHES

Paint your front-end loader. How about a control panel on the dashboard? See pages 72 and 74 for more ideas. Add paper-plate or construction-paper wheels. Draw a thick black line between them to look like caterpillar wheels.

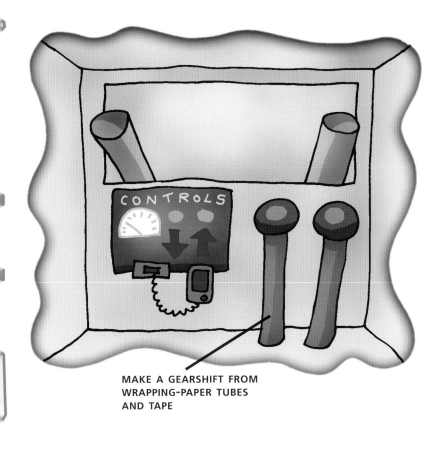

MAKE A GEARSHIFT FROM
WRAPPING-PAPER TUBES
AND TAPE

Mike Mulligan and His Steam Shovel by Virginia Lee Burton
The Night Worker by Kate Banks

How could you turn a chair, two brooms, and a plastic laundry basket into a front-end loader? Hint: Imagine the chair is the cab and you're using the basket as the bucket.

Paddle downstream in your very own canoe! Be sure to pack a tent and some supplies so you can set up camp on the shore. And don't forget the life preservers!

Here's What You Need

✔ Large cardboard box
✔ Utility knife (for grownup use only)
✔ Tape
✔ Extra cardboard

FINISHING TOUCHES
Aluminum foil or paint and paintbrushes; extra cardboard; 2 wrapping-paper tubes

MAKE YOUR CANOE!

1. Place the box horizontally, open side facing up. If necessary, cut down the sides so they are about 18" (45 cm) tall. If you need to make your canoe narrower, cut the box as shown; fold up the bottom and tape to secure.

2. Cut four curved triangle shapes out of cardboard as shown below.

3. Tape two triangles to the front sides and tape the front seam together to form the front of the boat, called the *bow*. Use the other two pieces to make the *stern* (the rear of the boat).

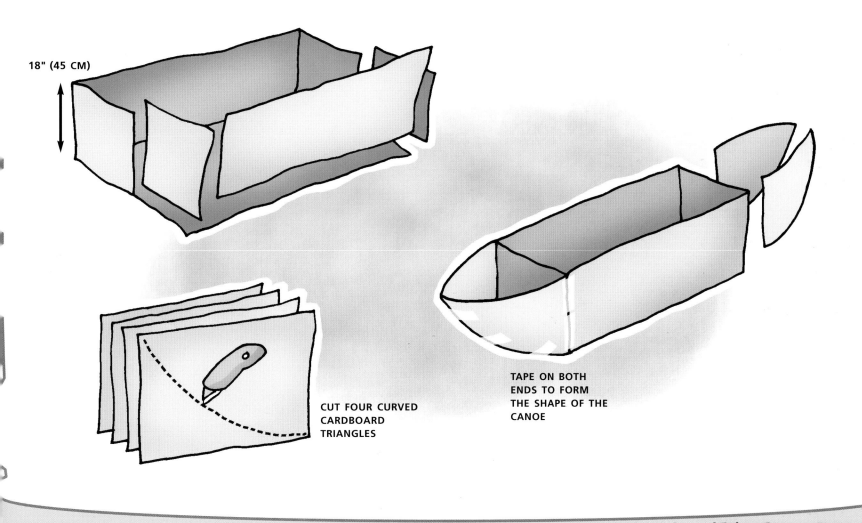

18" (45 CM)

CUT FOUR CURVED CARDBOARD TRIANGLES

TAPE ON BOTH ENDS TO FORM THE SHAPE OF THE CANOE

FINISHING TOUCHES

Lots of canoes are made from a shiny lightweight metal called *aluminum*. Wrap the sides of the box in aluminum foil to make a metal canoe. Or, paint your canoe your favorite color.

Cut a paddle shape out of cardboard and tape it to the end of a wrapping-paper tube.

IMPROVISE!

No wrapping-paper tubes for paddles? Try a broom! Can you think of anything else you could use?

Little Hands Story Corner™

Three Days on a River in a Red Canoe by Vera B. Williams

Covered Wagon

Load up your covered wagon and get ready to cross the prairie just like a pioneer! Or, just head to the GENERAL STORE (pages 108–110) to stock up on supplies.

Here's What You Need

✔ Large cardboard box
✔ Utility knife (for grownup use only)
✔ Tape
✔ 3 foam swim noodles
✔ Old sheet
✔ Extra cardboard
✔ Medium cardboard box

FINISHING TOUCHES
Rocking horse

MAKE YOUR COVERED WAGON!

1. Place the box horizontally, open side up. Cut off the front of the box as shown.

2. Tape the ends of the swim noodles securely to the sides of the box as shown.

Drape the sheet over the arches. Tuck it in and tape it in place to make it look neat.

3. Cut four large wheels out of cardboard and tape to the sides. Place the medium box inside the wagon for a bench.

FINISHING TOUCHES

Place the rocking horse in front of the wagon.

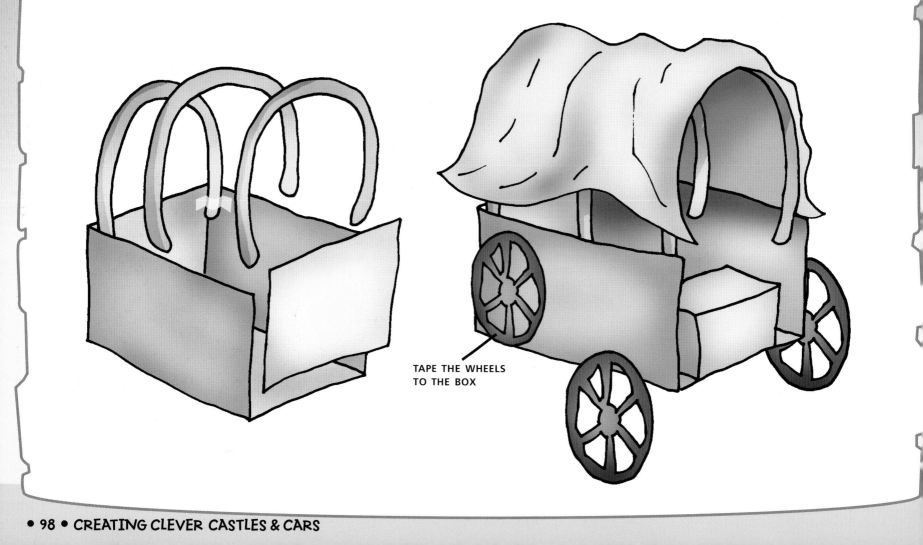

TAPE THE WHEELS TO THE BOX

Going West (My First Little House Books)
by Laura Ingalls Wilder

 IMPROVISE!

No swim noodles handy? What else would work to hold the sheet up? How about hula hoops?

No box? Turn a kid's play table upside down. How could you tape the noodles on to hold up the sheet?

All-Aboard Bus

CHALLENGE LEVEL 1 2

Do you travel by bus? Maybe you ride on a school bus or travel around town on a city bus. You can go anywhere you like on this bus!

Here's What You Need

✔ Large cardboard box
✔ Utility knife (for grownup use only)
✔ Extra cardboard (or save one of the box flaps)
✔ Tape
✔ Paper plates or disposable aluminum pie plates
✔ Metal fasteners or glue

FINISHING TOUCHES
Paper cup; pencil; cardboard scrap; recycled items for control-panel buttons and knobs (bottle caps, empty film canisters, etc.)

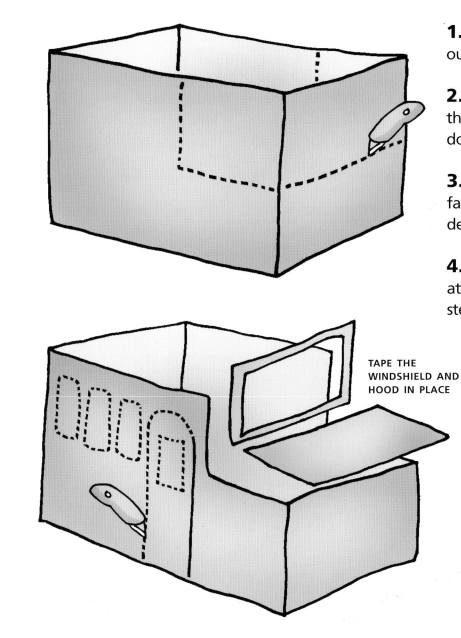

TAPE THE WINDSHIELD AND HOOD IN PLACE

MAKE YOUR ALL-ABOARD BUS!

1. Place the box horizontally, open side up. Cut a section out of the front as shown.

2. Cut a hood and a windshield out of cardboard and tape them in place. Cut out windows for the passengers and a door that swings open.

3. Attach paper-plate or pie-plate wheels with metal fasteners or glue. See CRUISING CAR, pages 70–72, for more decorating ideas.

4. For a steering wheel that turns, use a metal fastener to attach a paper or pie plate. Or, see page 72 for another steering-wheel idea.

FINISHING TOUCHES

For the ignition, cut a rectangular hole in the bottom of a paper cup. Trace around the top of the cup on the dashboard, cut out the circle, and push in the cup, leaving it free to turn. Cut a key out of cardboard. Glue buttons and dials onto your dashboard (see pages 72 and 74 for more ideas).

Don't Let the Pigeon Drive the Bus
   by Mo Willems
Bus Stops by Taro Gomi

MORE FUN!

● How about a school bus? Paint your bus yellow and add the name of your school in black letters. Don't forget the yellow lights on the front and the back of the bus! How about a small stop sign taped to a cardboard tube for the driver to hold out the window? Place small chairs or pillows inside the bus.

● Cut out most of the bottom of the box and cut small handholds below each window so you can travel along with your busload of passengers. Sing "The Wheels on the Bus" as you go!

What's for Sale?
Shops & Stands

It's fun to play store! How about making an old-fashioned general store that has a little bit of everything? Or an ice-cream cart with "homemade" treats?

Set up a pretend roadside stand that sells anything from flowers to fruit. Make some play money and you're all set for business! How many customers did you have today?

ICE CREAM

ICE-CREAM >CART<

CHALLENGE LEVEL 1

Dish it out! Go through the house or around the yard with your very own ice-cream cart. What flavors will you serve?

Here's What You Need

✔ Tape
✔ Small umbrella
✔ Small cardboard box
✔ Wagon
✔ Paint and paintbrush or markers
✔ Construction paper
✔ Child-safety scissors

FINISHING TOUCHES

Bell; chair (optional); small colored balls; glue; clean sponge; cardboard scraps; popsicle sticks

MAKE YOUR ICE-CREAM CART!

1. Tape the umbrella to the box.

2. Place the box inside the wagon. Paint a sign for the front. Decorate it with pictures of the ice-cream treats.

FINISHING TOUCHES

Hang a bell from the umbrella. Bring a chair if you want a seat!

Make some pretend ice-cream treats. Set a small plastic ball in a cardboard cone for an ice-cream cone. How many different flavors can you make? Glue a clean sponge between two pieces of cardboard — yum, an ice-cream sandwich! What could you glue onto a popsicle stick?

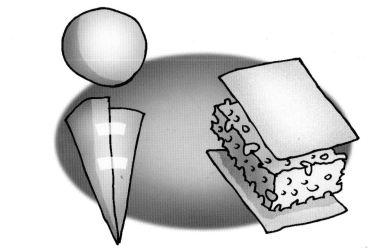

● Use a cooler instead of a box. With a grownup friend to help, fill it with ice and real ice cream and head off to visit the neighbors. What other supplies will you need?

Ice Cream Larry by Daniel Pinkwater
Ice-Cream Cones for Sale! by Elaine Greenstein

Don't have a wagon? Decorate the box to look like a cart. What could you use to make big wheels? How could you use an old skateboard to make your cart roll along?

CHALLENGE LEVEL 1 2

What's for sale at your pretend stand? How about flowers, fruit, stuffed animals, or ice-cold lemonade? Or, put your own original artwork on display!

Here's What You Need

✔ Large cardboard box
✔ Small cardboard box
✔ Utility knife (for grownup use only)
✔ Glue
✔ Sticks or wrapping-paper tubes

FINISHING TOUCHES

Paint and paintbrush or markers; construction paper; child-safety scissors; small chalkboard and chalk or poster board; small baskets; items to sell

Roadside Stand

BRYCE'S STAND

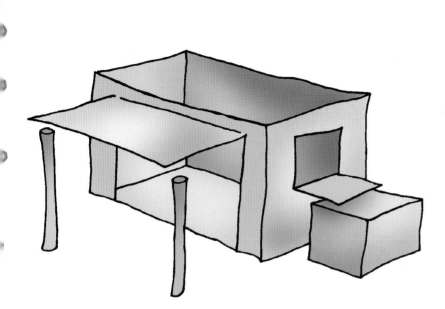

● Add groceries to sell. Cover empty boxes and other small containers with construction paper and decorate them with food labels.

● Decorate the inside of your store! Make props like a calculator and a phone. Glue small boxes together to make a cash register and fill it with construction-paper money.

MAKE YOUR ROADSIDE STAND!

1. Place the large box horizontally, open side up. Place the smaller box in the front, open side down. Cut out a window as shown, folding the flap down so it rests on the smaller box. Glue it in place.

2. Cut a door flap as shown, and prop it up with the sticks or the cardboard tubes.

FINISHING TOUCHES

Decorate a sign for your store and glue it over the window. How about a list of prices on a chalkboard or poster board? Display items for sale in the window and in baskets.

Little Hands Story Corner™

Alex and the Amazing Lemonade Stand by Liz and Jay Scott
Where Does Joe Go? by Tracey Campbell Pearson

General Store

GENERAL STORE

CHALLENGE LEVEL 1 2

Long ago, the general store sold a little bit of everything — from flour and sugar to fabric to rope and farm tools. It had to — it was the only store around!

Here's What You Need

✔ Large cardboard box
✔ Utility knife (for grownup use only)
✔ Ruler
✔ Tape

FINISHING TOUCHES

Paint and paintbrushes; stiff paper; chairs; 2 paper-towel tubes; extra cardboard

MAKE YOUR GENERAL STORE!

1. Place the box vertically, open end up. Cut 5" to 6" (12.5 to 15 cm) off three sides as shown to create a high front (save a piece of cardboard). Cut out a window.

2. To make western-style swinging doors, cut as shown.

3. Tape the piece of cardboard above the door for an awning.

FINISHING TOUCHES

Paint and decorate. How about some stripes on your awning? Make a construction-paper sign to hang above it. Set two chairs together to make a bench for your customers. Cut out a cardboard wagon wheel and put it out front. Use paper-towel tubes to prop open the window as shown on page 108.

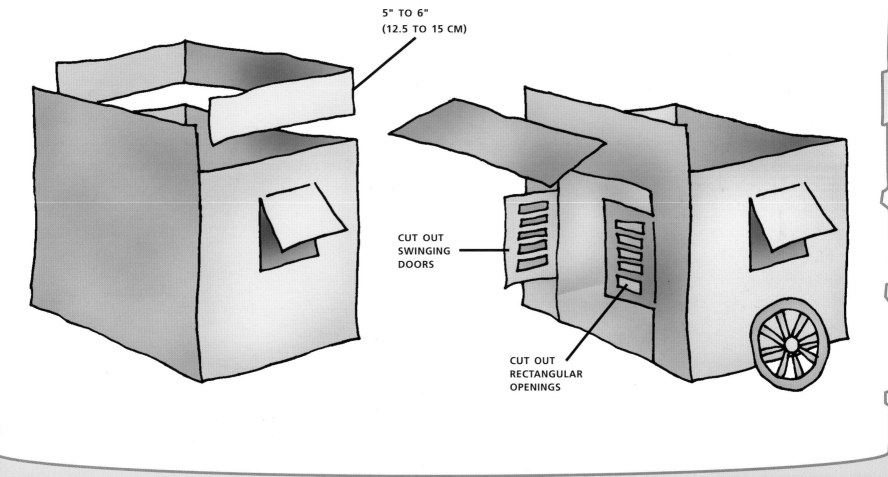

5" TO 6"
(12.5 TO 15 CM)

CUT OUT SWINGING DOORS

CUT OUT RECTANGULAR OPENINGS

MORE  FUN!

● Add goods to sell. Cover small boxes and cans with construction paper and decorate them with food labels.

● Make pretend money and a cash drawer (see ROADSIDE STAND, pages 106–107).

● What does a storekeeper wear? How about a big apron with the name of the store on it?

● Pretend you're a shopper. What will you need? Bring along a purse or wallet, some pretend money, and bags for your purchases. Don't forget your list!

Can you make a grocery cart out of a laundry basket and a chair, a wagon, or a baby stroller?

Little Hands Story Corner™

Ox-Cart Man by Donald Hall
The Marvelous Market on Mermaid by Laura Krauss Melmid

Would you happen to carry cell phone batteries?

BOB'S STORE

On with the Show!
Mini-Theaters & Places to Perform

Get ready to take center stage! Create a simple theater or even your very own circus tent. All you need is a doorway, a corner of the room, a table, or a big box.

With a group of friends or a cast of puppet characters, you're ready to act out your favorite stories or perform one-of-a-kind acts!

Doorway Theater

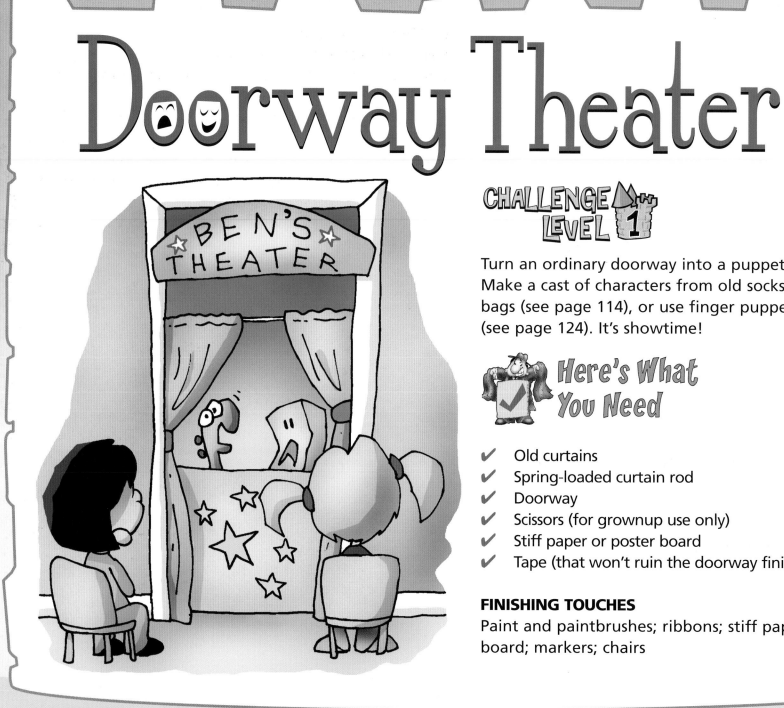

Turn an ordinary doorway into a puppet theater! Make a cast of characters from old socks or paper bags (see page 114), or use finger puppets (see page 124). It's showtime!

Here's What You Need

- ✔ Old curtains
- ✔ Spring-loaded curtain rod
- ✔ Doorway
- ✔ Scissors (for grownup use only)
- ✔ Stiff paper or poster board
- ✔ Tape (that won't ruin the doorway finish)

FINISHING TOUCHES

Paint and paintbrushes; ribbons; stiff paper or poster board; markers; chairs

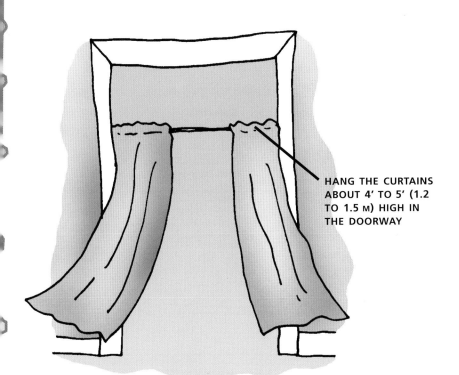

HANG THE CURTAINS ABOUT 4' TO 5' (1.2 TO 1.5 M) HIGH IN THE DOORWAY

FINISHING TOUCHES

Paint and decorate the theater. Cut two ribbons so you can tie back the curtains when it's time to start the show.

Cut a piece of stiff paper that's a little wider than the doorway. Decorate a sign with the name of your theater and tape it in place at the top of the doorway. Don't forget a sign to announce today's performance! Set up chairs for your audience.

MAKE YOUR DOORWAY THEATER!

1. Hang the curtains on the curtain rod. Secure the rod about 4' to 5' (1.2 to 1.5 m) high in the doorway.

2. Cut a piece of stiff paper or poster board so it's wider than the doorway. Tape it in place across the bottom of the door.

Lights Out! (Just for You! series) by Angela Shelf Medearis
Peppy's Shadow by Marcia J. Trimble
Make Your Own Puppets & Puppet Theaters
  by Carolyn Carreiro

MORE  FUN!

● Make sock and paper-bag puppets! Draw faces and clothes on paper lunch bags with markers. Or, glue fabric and paper scraps, yarn, and other decorations onto bags or old socks. To make finger puppets, see page 124.

● How about a ticket booth? Follow step 1 of the MARIONETTE THEATER (see pages 120–121). Don't forget a clock (see page 43) on the front to show the time of today's performance.

IMPROVISE!

Don't have a curtain rod and old curtains? What if you had some string, an old sheet, and two hooks or some sturdy tape instead?

Why of course you may have a raise in your allowance, son!

CHALLENGE LEVEL 1

Perform an amazing show right under your very own "big top"!

Here's What You Need

✔ 3 old sheets
✔ Table
✔ Tape (that won't ruin the finish on the table)
✔ Child-safety scissors
✔ Construction paper
✔ Plastic bottle

FINISHING TOUCHES

4 paper-towel tubes

CIRCUS TENT

MAKE YOUR CIRCUS TENT!

1. Fold two sheets so that they're the height of the table and tape them in place as shown. Leave an opening in front for a door.

3. To make the peaked roof, place the bottle in the center of the table. Cover with the third sheet (fold it under to fit the top of the table if necessary).

FINISHING TOUCHES

Cut flags out of construction paper and tape them to the paper-towel tubes. Tape them in the corners and in the center of the tent top.

2. Cut several pieces of construction paper in a scalloped pattern. Tape them around the edge of the table as shown on the finished tent.

MORE  FUN!

- Put on a circus! Dress up in your pajamas, borrow a pair of way-too-big shoes, and paint your face like a clown. What other circus costumes can you think up?

- Make a set of barbells by gluing a shoe box on each end of a cardboard wrapping-paper tube.

- Walk on "stilts" made from empty oatmeal containers and string.

- Put a rope or a line of tape across the floor. Can you walk the tightrope? How about a juggling show? Don't forget the hula hoops!

 **Learn More About It!**

See a live circus performance! Or watch a video or dvd of Cirque du Soleil, an amazing circus troupe from Canada.

Circus Girl by Tomek Bogacki
Mirette on the High Wire by Emily Arnold McCully
Olivia Saves the Circus by Ian Falconer

All you need to make this mini-theater is a corner of a room! How about acting out your favorite nursery tale, complete with scene changes? Or, make up your own story!

Here's What You Need

✔ Open corner of a room (without furniture)
✔ Tape (that won't ruin the surface of the wall)
✔ String and scissors (for grownup use only)
✔ Lightweight fabric

FINISHING TOUCHES
Paint and paintbrushes; large pieces of paper; clothespins; ribbons

CORNER STAGE

MAKE YOUR CORNER STAGE!

1. In the corner of the room, tape a piece of string from wall to wall above head height. Cut the fabric in half and hang the pieces over the string; tape them in back to hold them in place. Be sure you have room behind the curtains to move around.

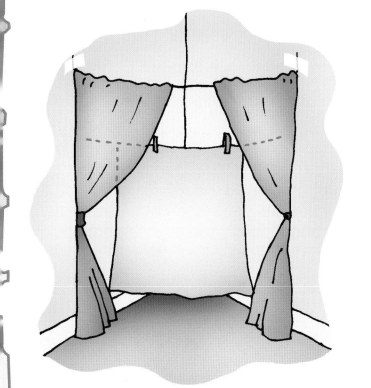

2. Hang another length of string inside the first one to hold your scenes. Make sure it's at a height you can reach so you can change scenes easily.

FINISHING TOUCHES

Paint a scene onto a large piece of paper. Use clothespins to hang it from the inner string. Make more scenes if you need them.

Cut ribbons to tie back the curtains on each side at the start of the show.

● Gather what you need for costumes and props. Store them behind the scenery for quick changes.

● Think about the character you're going to play. What does he or she wear? Will you have to walk a certain way or use a different voice?

Amazing Grace by Mary Hoffman

MARIONETTE THEATER

CHALLENGE LEVEL 1 2

It's fun to perform with marionettes — they move around on the stage while the puppeteer (that's you!) controls them from above. To make your own marionettes, see page 121. To make theaters for hand puppets, see DOORWAY THEATER (pages 112–114) and TWO-BOX THEATER (pages 122–124).

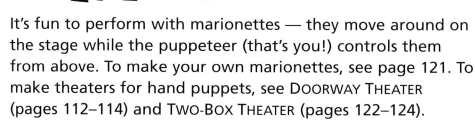

Here's What You Need

✔ Large cardboard box
✔ Utility knife and scissors (for grownup use only)
✔ Fabric
✔ Wooden pole
✔ Tape

FINISHING TOUCHES
Paint and paintbrushes; child-safety scissors; contact paper or construction paper; poster board; marker; metal fastener

NEXT SHOW

MAKE YOUR MARIONETTE THEATER!

1. Set the box vertically, open end down. Cut a door in the side and a window in the front.

2. Cut a small rectangle in the top of the box. Cut holes as shown below for the curtain pole.

3. Cut the fabric into two curtains to fit the window. Tape them so they hang from the pole.

FINISHING TOUCHES

Paint and decorate the theater. How about some stars cut from contact paper or construction paper? Make a clock face (see page 43) and glue it on the front to show the time of the next performance.

MORE FUN!

● Make marionettes from stiff paper! Dangle them through the slit in the top of the box.

ATTACH ARMS AND LEGS WITH METAL FASTENERS

TAPE STRINGS TO THE HANDS, FEET, AND HEAD

TIE THE STRINGS TO A CARDBOARD TUBE

CUT A SMALL HOLE ON EACH SIDE FOR THE CURTAIN POLE

Two-Box Theater

CHALLENGE LEVEL 1 2

You can change the scenery in this theater! Perform with sock or paper-bag puppets (see page 114) or finger puppets (page 124).

Here's What You Need

- ✔ Large cardboard box
- ✔ Utility knife, scissors, and yarn (for grownup use only)
- ✔ Medium cardboard box
- ✔ Tape
- ✔ Fabric

FINISHING TOUCHES

Child-safety scissors; construction paper; tape; wooden dowels or wrapping-paper tubes; paint and paintbrushes; markers; glue

MAKE YOUR TWO-BOX THEATER!

1. Place the large box vertically, open end down. Cut a door in the back or the side.

2. Place the medium box (open end down) on top of the large box. Cut an opening between the two boxes. Tape them together.

3. In the front of the top box, cut a window for the stage. Cut two curtains from the fabric and tape them to the inside of the window. Poke two holes as shown so you can tie back the curtains when you're performing.

4. In the top of the upper box, cut several slits for your scenery — they should be a little shorter than the dowels or tubes (see page 124).

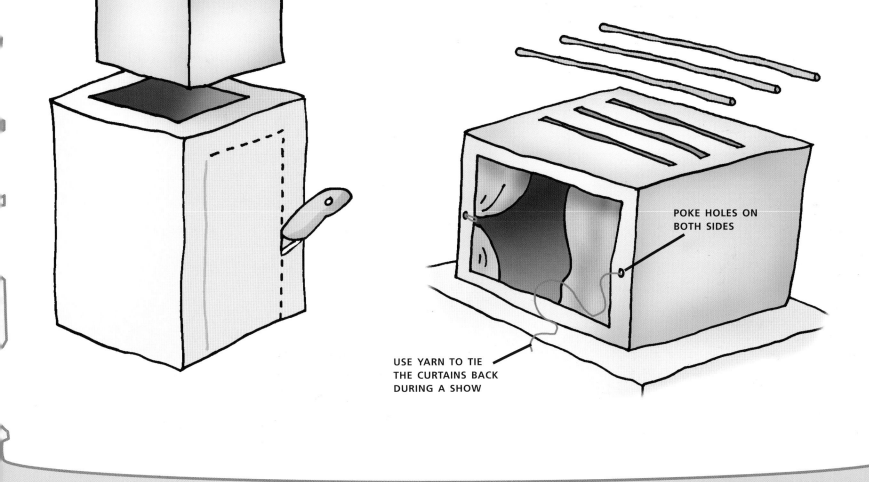

POKE HOLES ON BOTH SIDES

USE YARN TO TIE THE CURTAINS BACK DURING A SHOW

FINISHING TOUCHES

Cut pieces of paper the width of the top slits and draw background scenes. Tape the scenes to the dowels or cardboard tubes. Hang them from the top of the box in the order needed to act out your story.

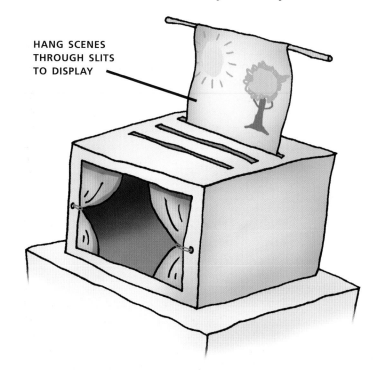

HANG SCENES
THROUGH SLITS
TO DISPLAY

Paint and decorate the theater. Make a sign that shows its name. And don't forget a sign to announce the upcoming performance!

● To make a ticket booth, follow step 1 of the MARIONETTE THEATER (see pages 120–121). Add a clock (see page 43) on the front to show the time of today's performance.

● Make finger puppets! Roll a strip of paper around your index finger and tape. Draw on eyes, nose and mouth, and glue on yarn hair. For sock or bag puppets, see page 114.

Resources

Where to see it and learn more about it …

ADOBE HOMES/PUEBLOS

http://www.indianpueblo.org/
http://www.GreatBuildings.com/buildings/
Taos_Pueblo.html
http://www.imagesofanthropology.com;
search Photographs for "pueblo"

ANCIENT EGYPT

http://www.GreatBuildings.com/buildings/
Great_Pyramid.html

ANIMAL HABITATS

About Birds: A Guide for Children by Cathryn Sill
Birds in Your Backyard by Barbara Herkert
Teaching Children about Backyard Birds by Catherine
Lazaroff
About Insects: A Guide for Children by Cathryn Sill
About Mammals: A Guide for Children by Cathryn Sill
To find a natural history museum near you:
http://www.ucmp.berkeley.edu/subway/nathistmus.html
To find a zoo near you: http://www.zoos-
worldwide.de/land/northamerica/northamerica.html

IGLOOS/INUIT CULTURE

http://www.GreatBuildings.com/buildings/Igloo.html
http://www.virtualmuseum.ca/Exhibitions/Inuit_Haida/
english.html
Building an Igloo by Ulli Steltzer
The Igloo by Charlotte and David Yue
Canadian Museum of Civilization, Ottawa;
http://www.civilization.ca/

PUPPETS & THEATER

Felt Wee Folk: Enchanting Projects by Salley Mavor
*Making Make Believe: Fun Props, Costumes, and Creative
Play Ideas* by MaryAnn F. Kohl

On Stage: Theater Games and Activities for Kids
by Lisa Bany-Winters
A Show of Hands: Using Puppets with Young Children by
Ingrid M. Crepeau and M. Ann Richards
Big Apple Circus, http://www.bigapplecircus.org/Home/
(to see a virtual tent raising, take an online big top
tour and more)

TRADITIONAL HUTS/AFRICAN CULTURE

http://www.imagesofanthropology.com
search Photographs for "African hut"
*Hands-On Africa: Art Activities for All Ages Featuring
Sub-Saharan Africa* by Yvonne Y. Merrill

TRANSPORTATION

U.S. Department of Transportation,
http://education.dot.gov/
National Air and Space Museum (Smithsonian Institution),
Washington, DC, http://www.nasm.si.edu/
To find an air and space museum near you:
http://www.aero.com/museums/museums.htm
NASA (National Aeronautics and Space Administration),
http://www.nasa.gov/home/
To find a railroad museum near you:
http://www.RailMuseums.com/
To find a maritime museum near you:
http://www.maritimemuseums.net/

> For more building projects and creative play-space
> ideas, visit www.marirutzmitchell.com

Activities by Challenge Level

FOR A DESCRIPTION OF THE THREE LEVELS, SEE PAGE 6.

Level 1

Bathtub Submarine 68
Circus Tent 115
Corner Stage 118
Cozy Cardboard House 12
Doorway Theater 112
Flower Fairy House 15
Ice-Cream Cart 104
Spider Web 48
Tricycle Taxi 66
Wiggly-Worm Tunnel 50

Level 2

Adobe House 21
A-Frame House 18
All-Aboard Bus 100
Big Stone Castle 39
Canoe 94
Clock Tower 42
Covered Wagon 97
Cruising Car 70
Dump Truck 76
Fire Engine 73
Front-End Loader 91
General Store 108
High-Flying Helicopter 82
"Icy" Igloo 28
Little Red Barn 36
Marionette Theater 120
Nesting Houses 24
Pirate Ship 84
Pointed Pyramid 44
Roadside Stand 106
Rocking Boat 86
"Roomy" Cardboard House 26
Soaring Spaceship 88
Traveling Train 79
Two-Box Theater 122

Level 3

Anthill 62
Beaver Lodge 57
Bird's Nest 54
Forest Log 60
Newspaper-Roll Hut 31
Underground Burrow 52

Index

A

adobe
    bricks, 23
    house, 21–23
A-frame house, 18–20
animal homes, 48–49, 50–51, 52–53, 54–56, 57–59, 60–61, 62–64
ant farm, 64
anthill, 62–64
appliances, cardboard kitchen, 14
astronaut
    costume, 90
    food, 90

B

barn, 36–38
bathtub submarine, 68–69
beaver lodge, 57–59
bird's nest, 54–56
boats, 84–85, 86–87, 94–96
bugs, making, 61
burrow, underground, 52–53
bus, 100–102
butterfly, clothespin, 61

C

calculator, 107
canoe, 94–96
car, 70–72
cardboard, crafts using
    animal homes, 52–53, 57–59, 62–64
    buildings, 36–38, 39–41, 42–43, 44–46, 75, 81
    houses, 12–14, 18–20, 21–23, 24–25, 26–27, 31–34
    theaters, 120–121, 122–124
    transportation, 68–69, 70–72, 73–75, 76–78, 79–81, 82–83, 84–85, 86–87, 88–90, 91–93, 94–96, 97–99, 100–102
    vendors, 104–105, 106–107, 108–110
cart, ice-cream, 104–105
cash register, 107
castle, 39–41
circus tent, 115–117
clock tower, 20, 42–43
construction vehicles, 76–78, 91–93
corner stage, 118–119

costumes

astronaut, 90
circus, 117
Egyptian, 46
fairy, 34
firefighter, 75
medieval, 41
mouse ears, 51
rabbit ears, 51
spider, 49
covered wagon, 97–99
crown
    Egyptian, 46
    medieval, 41
curtains, craft using, 112–114

D

dashboards, 72, 74, 93
doghouse, 20
doorway theater, 112–114
dump truck, 76–78

F

fabric, crafts using, 15–17, 50–51, 112–114, 115–117, 118–119
fairy
    house, 15–17
    wings, 17
finger puppets, 124
fire
    engine, 73–75
    station, 75
flower fairy house, 15–17
foam swim noodles, craft using, 97–99
front-end loader, 91–93

G

games, 30, 67
gas pump, 78
gearshift, 93
general store, 108–110
gingerbread house, 20
gravity, simulate lack of, 90

H

habitats. See animal homes
hat, princess, 41
helicopter, 82–83
houses, 12–14, 15–17, 18–20, 21–23, 24–25, 26–27, 28–30, 31–34
hula hoops, crafts using, 15–17, 50–51
hut, newspaper, 31–34

I

ice-cream cart, 104–105
igloo, 28–30
ignition switch, 102
insect homes, 48–49, 60–61, 62–64
insects, making, 61

L

lodge, beaver, 57–59
log, fallen, 60–61
lunar landscape, 90

M

marionette
    puppet, 121
    theater, 120–121
materials. See specific craft materials
milk jugs, craft using, 28–30
moon landscape, 90

N

nest, bird's, 54–56
nesting houses, 24–25
newspaper, crafts using, 31–34, 54–56, 57–59, 62–64

P

papier–mâché, crafts using, 60–61, 62–64
pirate ship, 84–85
plastic milk jug igloo, 28–30
princess hat, 41
puppet theaters, 112–114, 120–121, 122–124
puppets, 114, 121, 124
pyramid, 44–46

R

refrigerator, cardboard, 14
road signs, 67
roadside stand, 106–107
rocking boat, 86–87
rooms, cardboard houses with, 21–23, 26–27
rope, crafts using, 50–51, 66–67

S

school bus, 102
schoolhouse, 20
shield, 41
ships, 84–85, 86–87. See also canoe
sink, cardboard, 14
songs, 49, 64, 81, 102

spaceship, 88–90

spider web, 48–49
stage, corner, 118–119. See also theaters
stand, roadside, 106–107
stoplight, 67
store, general, 108–110
stove, cardboard, 14
string, crafts using, 15–17, 48–49, 118–119
submarine, 68–69

T

table, craft using a, 115–116
taxi, 66–67
theaters, 112–114, 118–119, 120–121, 122–124
ticket booth, 124
traffic signals, 67
train, 79–81
train station, 81
transportation. See boats; vehicles
treasure map, 85
tricycle, craft using a, 66–67
trucks, 73–75, 76–78
tunnel, worm, 50–51

U

underground burrow, 52–53

V

vehicles
    airborne, 82–83, 88–90
    wheeled, 66–67, 70–72, 73–75, 76–78, 79–81, 91–93, 97–99, 100–102, 104–105
vendors
    general store, 108–110
    ice-cream cart, 104–105
    roadside stand, 106–107
village, newspaper-hut, 34

W

wagon, covered, 97–99
wagon, craft using a, 104–105
web, spider, 48–49
wings, fairy, 17
worm tunnel, 50–51

More Good Books from Williamson

Welcome to Williamson Books! Our books are available from your bookseller or directly from Williamson Books at Ideals Publications. Please see the next page for ordering information or to visit our website. Thank you.

All books are suitable for children ages 3 through 7, and are 120 to 128 pages, 10 x 8, $12.95, unless otherwise noted.

ForeWord Magazine Children's Book of the Year Finalist
All Around Town
Exploring Your Community Through Craft Fun
by Judy Press

Early Childhood News Directors' Choice Award
Real Life Award
VROOM! VROOM!
Making 'Dozers, 'Copters, Trucks & More
by Judy Press
A Williamson Kids Can!® book for ages 5 and up

Sing! Play! Create!
Hands-On Learning for 3- to 7-Year-Olds
by Lisa Boston

Parents' Choice Gold Award
Fun with My 5 Senses
Activities to Build Learning Readiness
by Sarah A. Williamson

Animal Habitats!
Learning About North American Animals and Plants Thru Art, Science & Creative Play
by Judy Press

Parents' Choice Recommended
At the Zoo!
Explore the Animal World with Craft Fun
by Judy Press

Parents' Choice Approved
Fingerplays & Action Songs
Seasonal Rhymes & Creative Play
for 2- to 6-Year-Olds
by Emily Stetson & Vicky Congdon

Parents' Choice Approved
The Little Hands
Big Fun Craft Book
Creative Fun for 2- to 6-Year-Olds
by Judy Press

Parents' Choice Recommended
Early Learning Skill-Builders
Colors, Shapes, Numbers & Letters
by Mary Tomczyk

Parents' Choice Approved
Paper Plate Crafts
Creative Art Fun for 3- to 7-Year-Olds
by Laura Check

Kindergarten Success
Helping Children Excel Right from the Start
by Jill Frankel Hauser

Parents' Choice Recommended
Easy Art Fun!
Do-It-Yourself Crafts for Beginning Readers
(A *Little Hands*® Read-&-Do book)
by Jill Frankel Hauser

Parents' Choice Approved
Little Hands Create!
Art & Activities for Kids Ages 3 to 6
by Mary Doerfler Dall

Parent's Guide Classic Award
Real Life Award
The Little Hands ART BOOK
Exploring Arts & Crafts with 2- to 6-Year-Olds
by Judy Press

Little Hands® Celebrate America!
Learning about the U.S.A. through Crafts & Activities
by Jill Frankel Hauser

Wow! I'm Reading!
Fun Activities to Make Reading Happen
by Jill Frankel Hauser

Teachers' Choice Family Award
Parents' Choice Recommended
Sea Life Art & Activities
Creative Experiences for 3- to 7-Year-Olds
by Judy Press

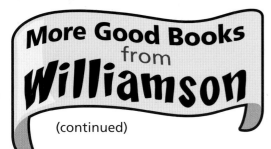

More Good Books from Williamson

(continued)

Parents' Choice Approved
The Little Hands Nature Book
Earth, Sky, Critters & More
by Nancy Fusco Castaldo

Around-The-World Art & Activities
Visiting the 7 Continents through Craft Fun
by Judy Press

The Little Hands Playtime! Book
50 Activities to Encourage
Cooperation & Sharing
by Regina Curtis

Math Play!
80 Ways to Count & Learn
by Diane McGowan & Mark Schrooten

American Bookseller Pick of the Lists
Rainy Day Play!
Explore, Create, Discover, Pretend
by Nancy Fusco Castaldo

Art Starts for Little Hands!
Fun Discoveries for 3- to 7-Year-Olds
by Judy Press

Early Childhood News Directors' Choice Award
Parents' Choice Approved
American Institute of Physics Science Writing Award
Science Play!
Beginning Discoveries for 2- to 6-Year-Olds
by Jill Frankel Hauser

Parent's Guide Children's Media Award
Alphabet Art
With A to Z Animal Art & Fingerplays
by Judy Press

For dinosaur lovers of all ages!
In the Days of Dinosaurs
A Rhyming Romp through Dino History
by Howard Temperley
(64 pages, $9.95)

Prices may be slightly higher in Canada

Visit Our Website!
To see what's new at Williamson and learn more about specific books, visit our secure website at:
www.williamsonbooks.com
or
www.Idealsbooks.com

3 Easy Ways to Order Books:
Please visit our secure website to place your order.
    Toll-free phone orders: 1-800-586-2572
    Toll-free fax orders: 1-888-815-2759
All major credit cards accepted (please include the number and expiration date).

Or, send a check with your order to:
    Williamson Books
    Orders, Dept B.O.B.
    535 Metroplex Drive, Suite 250
    Nashville, TN 37211

For large-volume orders or retail orders, please call Lee Ann Bretz at 1-800-586-2572.
Catalog request via mail, phone, or fax: see numbers and address at left.

Please add $4.00 for postage for one book plus $1.00 for each additional book.
Satisfaction is guaranteed, or full refund without questions or quibbles.